Modern Dance Forms

Ruth St. Denis
and Louis Horst

Photograph by
John Brefach

Modern

Dance Forms

in relation to the other modern arts

■ LOUIS HORST

CARROLL RUSSELL

A DANCE HORIZONS BOOK
Princeton Book Company, Publishers
Princeton, New Jersey

© 1961 by Louis Horst and Carroll Russell
© 1987 by Princeton Book Company, Publishers

Grateful acknowledgment is made
by Carroll Russell to Elizabeth Stille,
Shirley Genther and Sydney J. Harris for
advice in the presentation of the material;
by Marian Van Tuyl, Editor, to Doris Dennison,
Rebecca Fuller, Joanna Gewertz, Nik Krevitsky,
David Lauer, Eleanor Lauer and Bernice Peterson
for assistance in the preparation of the
manuscript for publication.

Production design by Lilly Weil Jaffe.

This is an unabridged republication of the
original edition, first published in 1961,
by Impulse Publications,
San Francisco, California

Princeton Book Company, Publishers
P.O. Box 57
Pennington, NJ 08534
ISBN 916622-52-5
Library of Congress Catalog Number: 61-11421
Printed in the United States of America

Cover photo by Barbara Morgan
Cover design by Design and Illustration

Contents

Grateful acknowledgment is made to the following:

to A. S. Barnes and Company, Inc. for permission to reprint a short passage from The Modern Dance by John Martin, copyright 1933, New York.

to Merle Armitage for permission to reprint two short passages from Modern Dance. Copyright 1935 by Merle Armitage. E. Weyhe, New York, publisher.

to Percy Lund Humphries and Co., Ltd., London, for permission to reprint two short passages from Sculpture and Drawings by Henry Moore, copyright 1944 by Curt Valentin, New York.

to Routledge & Kegan Paul Ltd., London, for permission to reprint a short passage from The Philosophy of Modernism by Cyril Scott.

to G. P. Putnam's Sons for permission to reprint two short passages from Twentieth Century Music by Marion Bauer. Copyright 1933 by Marion Bauer.

to Alfred A. Knopf for permission to reprint a short passage from New Musical Resources by Henry Cowell, copyright 1931, New York, and "The Cat and the Saxophone (2 A. M.)" from The Weary Blues by Langston Hughes, copyright 1929, New York.

to Liveright Publishing Corporation for permission to reprint two short passages from Expressionism in Art by Sheldon Cheney, copyright 1958, New York.

to the University of Chicago Press for permission to reprint a short passage from Plastic Redirections in Twentieth Century Painting by James Johnson Sweeney, copyright 1934 by the University of Chicago.

to Random House for permission to reprint "Epitaph on a Tyrant," from The Collected Poetry of W. H. Auden, copyright 1945 by W. H. Auden.

to New Directions for permission to reprint a short passage from Adventures in the Skin Trade by Dylan Thomas, copyright 1955, New York.

to Harcourt, Brace and Company for permission to quote two short phrases from Modern Building by Walter Curt Behrendt, copyright 1937, New York.

to Horizon Press, Inc. for permission to reprint a short passage from The Natural House by Frank Lloyd Wright, copyright 1954, New York.

to Rupert Hart-Davis for permission to reprint Brian Hill's translation of "Setting Suns" by Paul Verlaine from The Sky Above the Roof, copyright 1957, London.

to Humanities Press, Inc. for permission to reprint "Oread" by H. D. from Imagism and the Imagists by Glenn Hughes, published by the Stanford University Press, 1931.

Illustrations

Preface

Louis Horst was a man of great talent and boundless energy. He entered the world of modern dance as an accompanist at the Denishawn school in California. Soon, he was composing for some of this century's greatest dancers, including Graham, Humphrey, and Weidman. In addition, Horst was one of the first dance teachers to examine seriously the nature of modern choreography. He began teaching students in 1928 at the Neighborhood Playhouse, and his career continued until his death in 1964. Two of the courses that he created — *Pre-Classic Dance Forms* and *Modern Dance Forms* — survive today in the form of companion volumes reissued this year by Princeton Book Company's Dance Horizons imprint.

Horst's full schedule as performer, composer, editor, and dance composition teacher left him little time to write down what he taught. With determination and foresight, former student Carroll Russell took responsibility for capturing *Modern Dance Forms* in print. This volume contains articles written by Horst for the *Dance Observer* during the late 30s and 40s, with comments tape-recorded during Horst's classroom teaching (placed in the "Mr. Horst criticizes" sections of the text). First published in 1961, *Modern Dance Forms* accurately describes the course of study that educated thousands of professional dancers and actors from 1935 to 1964 under Horst's strict tutelage. With the growth of college dance departments in the 60s and 70s, this volume (and its companion *Pre-Classic Forms*) formed the basis for introductory courses in dance history and choreography. In this way, Horst's teachings have survived his own time to influence many generations of students and scholars.

Asked to assess his contribution to the theory of modern dance composition, Louis Horst replied, "A consciousness of the importance of form, and a survey of the textures and influences in all of the modern arts, and the relation of these to modern dance, specifically."[1] Horst's method for applying this theory draws from his view of dance as a "high art." His special ability to objectify, abstract, and formalize the highly subjective nature of dance began in his work as accompanist where his view from the keyboard gave him insight into the exact needs for making dances. His analytical mind and critical ability matched his musical sensitivity and nurturing capacity as a teacher. Supporting the growth of modern dance became his primary goal: "To see a great dancer or a great dance and be moved by it without knowing exactly why is the highest kind of communication, for that is kinesthetic communication."[2]

Interdisciplinary in approach, Horst's *Modern Dance Forms* focuses on the changing styles in other arts by first analyzing the elements of time, force, and space in movement. Horst then explores the sources of modern art, examining the stylistic characteristics of primitive, archaic, and medieval periods of art history. Having discussed the renaissance, baroque, and romantic periods in his book, *Pre-Classic Dance Forms,* Horst's next studies relate to "immediacies of contemporary life." Through this sequence, Horst prompts students of dance composition to experience contrasting styles while developing a keen eye and ear for emerging trends as a continual resource for dance ideas.

Louis Horst felt that the future of contemporary dance as an art form depended on skill and discipline of craft as well as natural talent, individualism, and tenacity. His sophisticated approach, documented in *Modern Dance Forms,* remains an important educational foundation for future generations of creative artists. Horst's survey of "isms" masterfully incorporates ideas and changing styles that emerged in art circles through the 1940s, giving history and substance to the art of modern choreography.

Today's students and teachers using this volume as a guide are encouraged to explore these 20th century idioms and additionally, experiment with new trends as they influence our contemporary thought. For example, "dada," "pop," and "op" art movements are natural extensions of Horst's cerebral studies. Minimalist performance art might be viewed as a further exploration of the primitive mode. "Neo-romanticism" is a natural outgrowth of expressionism.

For dance, Horst's analogy with the idiomatic styles of the other arts continues to give solid reference upon which to find a individual choreographic medium. Like the painter who experiments with Rouault's "palette knife" technique, or the composer who writes in

Schoenberg's "12-tone" style, Horst's teaching gives intellectual, experiential substance to the creative dance artist.

"To abstract a work is to sublimate it . . . it's getting the 'essence' of the gesture to give it importance and to give it an aesthetic pattern — that is what we are concerned with in art,"[3] Horst wrote in 1954. Incorporating new materials based on recent trends adds strength to this basic premise contained in *Modern Dance Forms,* and will enhance Horst's concept of dance as a fresh and vigorous adventure in art making.

Janet Mansfield Soares

[1]Coleman, Martha, "On the Teaching of Choreography. I. Interview of Louis Horst." *Dance Observer* XVI (9), p. 130.
[2]Horst, Louis, "Considers A Question," *Impulse 1954,* pp. 1, 6.
[3]Horst, *Op. Cit.*

Foreword

There come moments of honor and satisfaction in one's life but so seldom, and they come to me in this proportion.

This is in a sense an introduction to a book on a personal level, and perhaps an intimate level. It is a book I joyously welcome. The person who is responsible for its being is Louis Horst without whom modern dance in America would not be what it is today, and modern dance in any style all over the world would be without the magic of his imagination, his cruelty, his demonic will, and his skill. His first love and his last love is always dance and because of this all of us who are dancers, whether we entirely agree with him or not. . .to him we make obeisance and a deep gesture of gratitude for his passion and his love and his dream.

Introduction

Long before the time of recorded history dance must have been a developed and complex skill. Early man used it to help him surmount the riddles and tragedies of his daily life. He lived at the mercy of nature forces which we have learned to understand and in some degree to control, and dance was for him a powerful way to conciliate these forces. It was his religion and his poetry and his science. Ritual dances were his insurance of success against natural enemies of hunger, disease, and death — fertility dances, harvest dances, war dances. He danced to celebrate his joys in triumph or his sorrow in defeat, and believed that his very survival depended on a dance of such strength and agility that it would be worthy of notice by the gods who controlled his destiny.

Thousands of years of civilization have endowed us moderns with only a veneer of refinement to separate us from our crude and naïve ancestors. We accept unthinkingly the essential importance of communication between us marked by involuntary movements of hands, of eyes, of breath, etc., which express human emotions directly. We all have an instinct to use movement as a release for deep feelings of gratification ("I felt like jumping for joy") and frustration ("I was hopping mad"). Its elemental nature is conspicuous in the impulse to dance, so evident in every young child. The dancer's will has a relationship of intimacy with his body like the child's, whose demands, joys, and alarms are immediately told in physical movement. The dancer knows that his mind quickens his body and his body enlivens his mind, and he glories in the responsive obedience of one to the other. The feeling of oneness of body and spirit which is so obvious in the child must have been more nearly the condition of the primitive. We know, because provisions were left in his tomb to sustain the physical body on its trip to the after world, that the primitive's conception of immortality was unthinkable without his body. He did not relish the prospect of leaving

it behind to rot in a grave while the soul escaped to dwell in
austere purity.

Of this deep responsiveness between body and mind the art of
the dance is formed. Henri Bergson, in his essay "Laughter,"
has said of the artist (and it applies with special vividness to
the dancer) "He grasps something that has nothing in common
with language, certain rhythms of life and breath that are
closer to man than his inmost feelings, being the living law
— varying with each individual — of his enthusiasm and de-
spair, his hopes and regrets." This "something grasped" is
given form by the performing artist. It may be mounted on
a stage and offered to people who do not themselves possess
the rich power to discern these "certain rhythms of life." It
is built of symbols abstracted from daily living and intimately
associated in the memory of experience with action and emotion. To enjoy it, the trained eye of a connoisseur of painting
or the trained ear of a music lover are not needed. Any human
being who is willing to give it his attention should be enlivened
by dance.

Why is it then, that dance, with a venerable history and an
ability to speak with directness, is now considered as entertainment and that few write of it? Dance is not even recog-
nized by most aestheticians as an art. It is no longer an
essential of living, no longer qualifies as one of those things —
not bread — without which man cannot live. This is a very
new emphasis and arrangement of values in man's long history. When he fought for his existence against physical odds,
his body expressed his life directly and vividly. But the present day fellow who goes from down to up in an elevator, and
from here to there in an automobile, who does his hunting at
a desk or with a can opener, has a body that is nothing but a
shell which miraculously shelters the complicated biological
functions which keep him breathing. As abiding places for
our personalities, our awarenesses, our bodies are dishon-
ored and atrophied with disuse.

Words serve us where actions once did. No wonder modern man has forgotten what gratification it once was to him to express his participation in life in disciplined movement. One has only to look at the proud posture of the trained dancer — the carriage of his spine and his head — to sense his enjoyment in the knowledge of power in bones and muscles. But lacking this knowledge of power, most people respond to the concert dance as to a language only half understood, and their fears of the unfamiliar are more acute than fears of the novel in the other arts.

The dance as an art form, like an easel painting or a mounted piece of sculpture, is a fairly new phenomenon. Even the ballet, which was the first dancing to be presented in the Western World as spectacle, grew out of court performances in which the king and queen and the ladies and gentlemen-in-waiting made up both cast and audience. Folk dancing, social dancing, still are widely enjoyed as forms of self-entertainment. The principal connotation of dance, therefore, is of physical stimulation and emotional release through action. But any present-day concert dance production, although it does accomplish this effect through an automatically sympathetic physical response in the audience, also proffers emotional refreshment and intellectual quickening. To many, at first, this seems highly inappropriate to dancing.

Because of the inferior status of dance in the culture of the Nineteenth Century, the rebellion against outmoded forms in the dance world didn't appear until the other modern arts were somewhat established. The manner and the reasons for the rebellion are strikingly similar, however, to what occurred with painters, sculptors, musicians and poets. Although there are scores of books about the visions and values in the other modern art fields, little has been written to explain the techniques of the dance as a means of aesthetic communication.

Definition of the Modern Dance

The year 1920 is usually given for the appearance of an established new dance in Germany. Quite independently, nearly ten years later great changes occurred in this country. Martha Graham gave her first concert in 1926. John Martin's The Modern Dance, published in 1933, was almost the first book written on the subject here, and he describes at this late date the familiar pattern shown in the other arts many years before. "In carrying out this purpose (the expression of an inner compulsion) it has thrown aside everything that has gone before and started all over again from the beginning."

Isadora Duncan preceded this new dance and has been thought of as the founder of the modern dance movement. Actually she was an isolated phenomenon — a performer of great genius, the originator of a short-lived intensely romantic kind of dance, and the victim of a mass of embarrassingly sentimental imitators. But certain of Duncan's tenets and practices were an impetus toward what was to come. First, she made a complete break from the academic, repudiating its traditional costumes, decor, music, technique. And second, by discarding her shoes, her feet, instead of being a point of escape from reality as in the ballet, became the essential contact with the life-charged earth.

The founders of the present modern dance turned away from two forms: the dry technicalities of the ballet, and the vague formlessness of the "interpretative" dance. The principal reason for the lag in opening of this field to new ideas in comparison to their appearance in the other arts has been the frightening intimacy of the instrument used. The instrument, the body, is the very definition of intimacy. To use it in new ways for the expression of artistic ideas calls for more courage than to brush paint on canvas in new ways. The dancer's instrument, his raw material, has more personal and limiting associations in the inner mind of his audience than color, tone, texture, shape, or even words can have.

The pioneers in modern dance and their successors recaptured the relation that the primitive has to his body — an intimacy with the muscle tensions of daily movements which had been lost to modern men. This is not at all the ballet dancer's awareness of line, of speed or balance, and dramatic portrayal of a role. It is, rather, an inner sensitivity to every one of the body's parts, to the power of its whole, and to the space in which it carves designs. The great quest was to find ways to attain this sensitivity, and manners in which to discipline it for communication. In the beginnings of discovery of new forms, the dancers did not trust themselves with the distractions of musical accompaniment, elaborate costume, or decor. The dances were apt to be solos and were usually performed with a rhythmic background of percussion or simple sounds. Gradually, as the path ahead became more clear, theatrical complements such as lighting, settings and costumes were added to intensify the projection of the movement.

Mary Wigman, the great figure in German dance, described her early problem in these words: "The learned form was no longer decisive for the dance as an art, but the content itself, seeking a form of expression, endeavored to create one for itself." Martha Graham in this country felt that her dance must move to America's pulse. "It is a characteristic time beat, a different speed, an accent, sharp, clear, staccato." The researches and experiments of Doris Humphrey in the Thirties brought her to a dance form which was of full theatre dimensions. It did not tell a story, but took its own elements of space, dynamics and rhythm, and molded them into a structure which belonged to them alone.

There is an extraordinary similarity in the desired end and in the development of a modern dance in the two separated centers of creative work (Germany and America). The dissimilarity is perhaps to be the expected one resulting from differences in cultural surroundings. The Wigman dance, characteristic of German culture, was concerned principally with the relationship of man to his universe. Mary Wigman conceived of space as a factor, like time, with which to compose. The emphasis was thus taken off the body of the dancer and put onto the idea which the dance wished to make manifest. The American Dancer, living in a new, developing country, did not feel the enmity of limiting space, was less conscious of his use of it. His subject matter was chiefly an objective comment on his people and his times.

Both built up the art form by abstracting familiar everyday movement. The realistic gesture or posture is taken as a point of departure on which to construct a poetic metaphor. The movement then becomes a symbol and arouses emotion in the audience through recollection — an echo of emotion without the limitation and particular directions that that emotion had in experience. The response to a dance greatly conceived and greatly performed is in that inner primitive, intuitive region where lies the whole man. This is the source of all art appreciation and the dancer must so perfect his sensitivity of body and mind that he can reach it by way of the poetic sense.

A bewildering variety of methods of body training have grown up. There are as many physical techniques as there are performer-teachers. Instead of the universal ballet principle of a secure powerful center of gravity in an upright back from which the brilliant movements of arms and legs give an unreal and superhuman impression, the modern dancers talk of movement based on the principles of "tension and relaxation," "fall and recovery," "contraction and release." The flexibility and shift of movement to various parts of the body give it a range of expression as wide as life experience.

The jagged rhythms of modern music, the often jangled colors and shapes of painting, the bristling abrupt quality of much sculpture, the striving in architecture for a response to the active, moving needs of daily life; all these qualities reflect the Twentieth Century's aggressive conquest of physical things. Modern dance achieves like qualities through techniques that train the body to change dynamics with speed and a visible tension. All the other arts are driven to try to infuse movement and speed into their work in order to reflect the pulse of the times. The dance, when it chooses, can be the direct embodiment of these phases of Twentieth Century living. Whereas in the classical ballet tension is denied, in the modern dance it is exploited to the fullest.

This art has infused movement with a vibrant, strong texture effected largely through a use of dissonance. It does not depend on beautiful line, unearthly balance, or sexual titillation. The movement is abstracted to express in aesthetic form the drives, desires, and reactions of alive human beings. It does not have to do with fairies or ghosts or toys come to life, except as they might exist in the mind of an alive human being. Consider the role of "Giselle" beautifully danced. One is moved by the purity of line, by the breath-taking accuracy of the movement. And there is much more; there is the sensitiveness to a characterization of an innocent and injured young girl, which is akin to the portrayal of a great actress. Now consider in contrast the role of the young wife in Martha Graham's Appalachian Spring. This too is a composition with clear cut characters, and a story situation. The dancing of this role, though it is done with extraordinary skill, never gives us satisfaction in the mere witnessing of this skill, or even in sympathy for the character, but by revealing through movement the tender womanhood of all such young wives since the world began.

The moderns discarded in one gesture all the procedures of the previous theatre dance — the inevitable pattern of revolution.

The ballet, changing gradually from the days of Fokine's innovations, seems in an evolutionary way to be surmounting its mountain of tradition. The successful ballet choreographers such as Balanchine, Tudor, Robbins, and DeMille, appear more and more liberated from the classic rules, and from the traditional ballet aloofness, and free to accept tensions and dissonances which put their work in touch with contemporary life. With an increased reliance on theatrical effects (setting, costuming, lighting) on the part of modern choreographers, the two styles of dance, poles apart thirty years ago, are, at least in surface aspects, approaching one another.

There is a kind of presentation which runs more or less conspicuously through all the modern arts. It might be added to the other "isms" descriptive of new styles, with the name "suggestivism." An idea is touched upon in the briefest fashion like an insect which lights briefly on a leaf before flying on to the next. The poets use words suggestingly, disjointedly; the reader does the developing in his own imagination. Many painters put images on their canvases suggestive of reality, but only lightly indicated. In dance, traditional pantomime is the opposite of suggestivism. There, although not in the context of real experience, the motions of real experience are reproduced. Modern dancers use pantomime very sparingly. Instead, by the merest flash of suggestion reminiscent of mood or real experience, they lead the spectator to develop the idea with the help of his own associations.

A true dancer has a temperament which directs him to express feelings and ideas through moving the body in space. This instinct must be greatly enhanced by training so that he not only has a strong co-ordinated instrument, but an immediate impulse to translate his comments and reactions into rhythms, muscular dynamics and spatial arrangements. He will recognize that a protected person, a nun for instance, has a posture of non-aggression: center of gravity back on the heels; an insecure, hunted person's body weight is constantly shifting, ready for flight: the ambitious, go-getter type is, of course, thrown forward. Body postures typical of character traits may be narrowed to the dimension of the carriage of the head or the walking gait — the really observant eye can detect character without communication from face or speech.

Contrary to common belief ("my five-year-old could do that") creative artists today proceed with deep study and rigorous training. As Paul Klee put it, "One must know a great deal and be able to do a great deal, while creating the impression of its being innate, instinctive." Henry Moore, although his forms are only vaguely representational of human forms, still practices drawing from life. He says it keeps him "visually fit" and "enlarges his form repertoire." Ten years is the generally accepted period of training and experience necessary to make the dancer's body into a competent instrument. Because there is no standard curriculum to teach the new language of movement, each dancer must largely discover his means of communication for himself. To do this, all his seeing, hearing and thinking must be pointed according to that language.

In addition to this complete dedication to his career as a performer, the modern dancer who is a creative artist is also a choreographer. His technique has much more than virtuoso significance to him, for it must be the purveyor of his ideas. As in the other arts of today, there are very few rules for him to go by as a designer of dances. Theories of dance composition have been formulated and taught only in the last thirty years, and almost nothing has been written on the subject. There is therefore little except the devious and long way of experience to help the talented beginner to find a style of gesture, a character of line, a dynamics of movement appropriate to his idea. The succeeding discussions are designed to help him choose forms which will give his work convincing dignity.

The divisions are titled in strictly qualified terms, but in spite of the type-names used, it must be understood that they are not intended to be precise or exclusive. One cannot build a rigid wall around this or that growth. Modern art is a free art and refuses to live within any boundaries. The styles in modern choreographic forms to be described later should be taken as suggestive, not definitive.

First Rules of Composition

PREREQUISITE TO ANY CHOREOGRAPHY

To compose is not an inspirational experience. Composition is based on only two things: a conception of a theme and the manipulation of that theme. Whatever the chosen theme may be, it cannot be manipulated, developed, shaped, without knowledge of rules of composition. In the fervor of new styles of movement and new subject matter, some modern dancers have been guilty of neglecting these fundamental rules, and so have regrettably weakened their work. The laws which are the basis on which any dance must be built should be so familiar to the choreographer that he follows them almost unconsciously.

As Susanne Langer has said, "Nothing has an aesthetic existence without form. No dance can be called a work of art unless it has been deliberately planned and can be repeated." The word "compose" implies posing or placing some parts of a whole in relation to other parts. In music this order, this plan, creates a tonal structure, in dance a visual one. The basic rules by which such a structure is devised have remained unchanged throughout Western history and can be learned by anyone.

One way for the dancer to absorb indelibly the simple mathematical conception of basic rules of form is to work with and through the music of the Pre-Classic period. The Fifteenth, Sixteenth and Seventeenth Centuries represent a formal era in Western history and it will be found that music written for the court dances of these times embodies the strict form that should be helpful to the contemporary student. It is good discipline to compose studies paralleling the musical structure of these dances. They should be sufficiently short and sufficiently clear in design to teach the lesson in strict form. The diverse rhythms, tempos and moods of the Pre-Classic dances present the possibility of very wide variety of emotional content, too. For instance, the Pavane lends itself to ideas of pride, power; the Galliard to gaiety; the Courante to studies in running movements: pursuit, for instance, or play, or the continuous motion of a machine. The Allemande suggests the sentimental, or the flowing: dances of affection, solicitude. The impelling tempo of the Gigue demands exciting movement which may be frenzied, tight, or frightened; the Minuet the smallest possible: timid and hairsplitting. But within these emotional expressions there is always the hard and mathematical core of the framework.

The most deeply instinctual aesthetic form is the A B A: a beginning, a middle and an end. This is the universal pattern of life itself: we are born, we live, we return to the unknown. It is the three part form which is the rhythm of the natural drum beat, the pattern of the common limerick verse, and also the usual basis of serious musical composition of any dimension, from a simple song to a complex symphony.

The first theme is stated in the A and manipulated; B is a contrasting theme, and after its manipulation the finish is a return to A probably in a somewhat different aspect. It is necessary for the composer at the outset to state the thematic materials (which derive from his idea) simply and clearly. They must be selected with judgment so that they are not only striking, but will lend themselves to manipulation. The theme is like a seed containing the germ for the development that is to follow. A barren theme, that is one which resists development, is difficult to describe, but with experience one learns to recognize it. The statement of the theme will usually consume about one quarter of the length of the whole section. The remainder consists in manipulation of the movement elements of that theme through several different devices. Repetition is one of the first laws of manipulation; inversion is another, or there can be amplification or contraction. The choreographer is free to develop one movement of the theme more than the others. If one element is a diagonal gesture, any of the four diagonal directions are eligible for variety's sake. Tempo and rhythm can be changed, too, so long as the choreographer cleaves to basic movements of his original theme.

Material introduced for the theme of B should be fresh and contrasting. For instance, if A includes a turn, do something in B which does not turn. If forward movements appear in the original theme focus toward the floor in the secondary one. The B section is less important than the A, but it is necessary to provide variety, to avoid monotony. The simple overall form A B A can be enlarged with the addition of a C into a four part form A B C A or the more interesting five part forms: A B C A B or A B C B A. C is a subsidiary idea, often just a transitional one.

A form quite unrelated to the A B A form is theme and variations. Here there is a statement of a theme of some length, say eight measures, upon which any number of variations can be built in completely different styles so long as the thematic material is always indicated. The latitude allowed in this varying on a theme is much wider than the manipulation consistent with the A B A form. For instance, a forward movement may be given in a version of hopping, crawling, pointing or merely looking, forward. A turn may appear as a violent spinning or only an evidence of a desire to turn. Dramatically the theme and variations presentation of an idea is inevitable with certain material; for instance, Charles Weidman's dance composition On My Mother's Side portrays variations on the theme of the family. A composer could spend his life drawing upon the endless variations that are hidden in any good theme. Some painters produce scores of pictures which are variations on a favorite idea — Cezanne's apples. William Faulkner, in almost his whole output of writing, dwells upon the same theme.

The <u>Rondo</u>, another completely independent form, can be pictured: A B AC A D A E A F A —. It provides for different material in each of the alternate parts: B, C, D, E, etc., but they must always be tied together by a recognizable but not necessarily exact return to A, the central theme. For instance, a dance of boredom might portray an individual's attempt to escape through play, love, religion — but always after each trial returning to the boredom represented by the A theme. Martha Graham's history-making solo dance <u>Frontier</u> is in rondo form. The pioneer woman, at first posed against the fence of her homestead, is shown in various occupations of her frontier life. After each, she returns to the contemplation of her vast world from the original position which is related to the fence piece.

In <u>The Homophonic Forms of Musical Composition</u> Percy Goetschius has laid down rules of composition for musicians. With slight changes in a word here and there, five of them apply equally well to judgments on the part of the choreographer.

    1. Is the work sufficiently beautiful and is its movement delineation striking and ingenious?

    2. Is the <u>formal</u> <u>design</u> rational and clear?

    3. Is its <u>rhythmic</u> <u>structure</u> distinct and effective?

    4. Does <u>it contain</u> <u>sufficient</u> fullness?

    5. Is the demand of <u>contrast</u> adequately respected, and the bane of <u>monotony</u> avoided?

The preceding emphasis has been on an almost mechanical devising of the structure of any work of art. A mathematical analysis of form, however, does not deny that the gifted artist has in addition an instinct for beautiful line, for the

selection of the most effective gesture or quality of movement. The creative imagination which guided Braque's subtle
feel for color, Tolstoy's special sense of proportion, or
Stravinsky's sensitivity to rhythm, cannot be taught. All
these artists came to the full expression of their gifts, however, through a mastery of the use of rules of form. Thorough
understanding of the nature of strictest form should be part
of any would-be choreographer's equipment as surely as the
painter should be able to paint a rose, no matter what liber-
ties with realism he may later find necessary. Also, in actual
practice, experienced artists consciously break the tenets of
strict form. They take "poetic license." But the beginner
must have the laws just discussed in his blood stream so that
he is never without the feeling of the necessity of form even
though the rules are somewhat flexible. He is then ready to
study more specifically the kind of movement, the style of
gesture which he will draw upon when he composes dances of
the contemporary world.

THE PRACTICE OF MODERN

DANCE FORMS

The Elements of Dance

UNDERSTANDING BY CONTRAST

The old general laws of compositional form remain the same — laws which govern structure, unity, proportion, emphasis, sequence. It is the <u>style</u> in their application which changes. Nowadays there are new languages of expression which give a texture that is the very definition of "modern" in each art.

Before examining the different styles in which modern dancers now express their ideas, the basic elements out of which all dance is made will be discussed. The present interpretation of these age-old elements will be better understood if it is contrasted with the practices of the Nineteenth Century romantics, and if frequent analogies are made between one field of art and another.

The elements of any of the arts are sufficiently similar and overlapping to cause a good deal of borrowing of terms between them. For instance, we speak of tone "color," melodic "line," the "rhythm" of a painting, "dissonance" of color or of movement, "discordant" building styles, or an "architectonic" literary style. However, there are only three arts

whose basic existence is dependent upon, and conditioned by
time duration: poetry, music and dance. The elements of
music — melody, rhythm and harmony — are the most closely
analogous to those of dance. It is music, therefore, which
will most frequently be referred to in an effort to clarify the
differences which mark off the modern dance from the traditional Nineteenth Century style and which will reveal the
nature of the elements of modern dance.

Melody is linear in essence. It forms the contour, the outline, of music, and so corresponds to line in dance. Rhythm
in the two arts is identical. It is a perpendicular breaking
up of the material of melody into pulses, forward-moving
in time duration. Harmony, defined as simultaneous tone
relationship, tonal color, inner activity, is similar to the
texture of dance movement; that inner muscular quality which
is the physical essence of movement.

Space Design

If melody in music is defined as relating to the profile, the
outer shape, with no thought of an inner physical quality, in
dance it has to do with movement delineations in space — the
contour, the outline — and not with any inner muscular-
physical quality.

The source of musical melody has always been the scale.
For three hundred years melodic material of composers nearly always had been drawn from the two diatonic modes (major
scale joyous, minor scale sad). These led inescapably toward
the symmetrical and predictable, especially the major which
is formed of two even tetrachords: two whole steps and then
one half step.

two tetrachords

The progressive composers of today have sought richer sources for their melodies than were offered by these over-worked modes. They borrow from other times and peoples, and they invent untried combinations of notes. Just as all the modern arts struggled to escape pedestrian rhythms, so they all sought a fresh freedom and vitality in more striking linear design, whether it was a Brancusi, a Satie, a Corbusier, an E. E. Cummings, or a Mary Wigman.

The first experimenters in music turned for new sources to the scales of older cultures. The pentatonic scale of the primitive races has only five tones: d, e, g, a, b, and sounds open and less symmetrical in our ears. The whole-tone scale with its six evenly spaced intervals: c, d, e, f#, g#, a#, has a planal, two-dimensional quality. The Greek and medieval modes carry a suggestion of taut, sparse line.

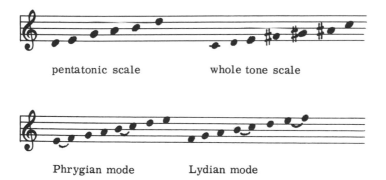

pentatonic scale   whole tone scale

Phrygian mode   Lydian mode

The linear and spatial designs of modern painting, sculpture, and the new dance (each in its own way) were all strongly influenced by the urge to apprehend the cultural aspects of the art of the primitive, the archaic and the medieval periods that were reflected in these modes.

Modern musicians explored melodic devices still further. They created a new dissonant effect by writing two melodic lines in different tonalities (bi-tonality), also writing three or more tonal lines in different tonalities (poly-tonality). And finally, melodic material is today often fashioned by them from the twelve notes of the octave used without any suggestion of tonality (atonality). While not so scientifically tabulated, the other arts also approximate these linear qualities in their new designs on canvas or in space.

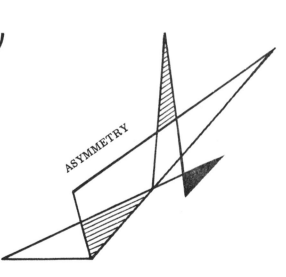

SYMMETRY

In music the use of modal, bi-tonal, and atonal melodic material produced a strong and virile counterpoint (one melody
attended by one or more related but independent melodies):
free and dissonant. This linear development was largely due
to the fact that modal melodies defy satisfactory harmoni-
zation. The importance of the drawing away from tonality
(mood) and the harmonic concept of music (more mood) toward a free dissonant counterpoint, cannot be overestimated.
Without doubt it has influenced the dance in its use of free,
asymmetric, striking space-patterning.

It was some time, however, before the first dancers, pioneer-
ing in new forms, became aware of the fresh use of the pentatonic scale by Bartok and Kodaly, of the whole-tone melodies
of Debussy, Rebikoff and Cyril Scott, of Satie's employment
of the archaic Greek modes, and Koechlin's treatment of the
medieval modes, of Milhaud's and Casella's bi-tonality and
Schoenberg's atonal writing. The once curved line straight-
ened out and movement designs achieved strange and striking
results. Gone were the predictable space patterns so fami-
iar in "Liebestraum" or "To a Wild Rose."

To "understand by contrast" one needs only superficially to
compare a melodic line of any romantic composer with one
by Paul Hindemith, the plastic organization of a Renaissance
painting with that of a Picasso, the Venus de Milo with an
Archipenko, the space design indicated in a picture of any
Nineteenth Century dancer with that projected in a photograph
of Martha Graham.

Of course, composers still write symmetrical melodies, and
the dancer, too, can employ symmetry. In his first studies
it is wise for him to avoid it entirely, but also to avoid the
mistake of relying upon the grotesque for its own sake. The
aim here is to destroy the tyranny of the symmetric in linear
design; to use asymmetry as a truly new speech.

DANCE STUDY IN STRANGE SPACE DESIGN

The dancer is advised to explore the space about him for new and strange designs in both pose and action; for new delineations of movement in space; for design which will get away from what Doris Humphrey described as the static quality of symmetry. Strange space design is achieved in the body by forswearing the symmetric in gesture or in posture; one shoulder higher than the other, hands at different angles, knees focused in different directions, a feeling deep throughout the whole body of distortion and strangeness. There should be no natural walks or leaps, no predictable sequence.

A second recommended dance study in Strange Space Design is an experiment with movement which consciously measures out planes in space. Each part of the body is aware every moment of where it is in respect to all parts of the body and with respect to the audience. There is no quality or idea contained here, no emotion involved. This is just a muscular experiment.

Each of the following sections of the modern forms study will have a brief musical composition appropriate for use as accompaniment in that particular style. The four pieces suggested here are examples of four tonal modes of writing: with the whole tone scale, using two keys (bitonal), using no key (atonal), and in the pentatonic scale. They should provide a background which will help the dancer discover the strange, taut and asymmetrical body movement.

"Yellow Alphabet" from <u>Allegory</u> — Danced by Arlene Laub
Choreography by Alwin Nikolais   Photograph by David S. Berlin

Ganztonleiter-Melodie

Whole Tone Scale

Lothar Windsperger

Ruhig gehend (Andante)

Zweitonales Stückchen

Rechte Hand C dur
Linke As dur — Bitonal

Lothar Windsperger

Mäßig, sehr ausdrucksvoll (Moderato, espressivo assai)

Nordiſches Lied
(5 ſtufige Tonleiter)

Pentatonic Scale

Lothar Windſperger
Op 37 1. Heft

Louis Horst

Mr Horst Criticizes Dance Studies in STRANGE SPACE DESIGN

You only rolled over. Move like a sphere in space.
Never lose the planal concept.

Complete control!
Tension!
Here is the value — plus the fact it makes strange design.

Measured out — not free wheeling.

You always have to know where you're going — how things look to the audience.
You must do the impossible. A dancer is an aesthetic acrobat — must be —
so you can do anything you want to do.

The power of slow motion. We see the thing happening.

Don't dangle!

If you don't feel that your foot's in the right place you may need a mirror
or someone to tell you until you do it intuitively.

A quarter of an inch makes a difference — that sort of exactitude that
makes it professional. Nothing casual should happen on stage anyway.

I'm being strict as hell, but you have to be
that way with yourself sometime.

When you get it, it's an effective design.

No emotion — cold design — but it may convey emotion through its tensions.

Don't do willow stuff — slower and more coordinated.

I know it hurts. You didn't think it was going to be fun, did you?
Dance and be happy?

Rhythm

Although the word rhythm has a variety of definitions and describes recurrences of more or less regularity in widely different phenomena — design, history, behavior, etc., the meaning we are here concerned with refers to specific recurrence of time duration.

Metric regularity of pulse is the life-blood of poetry, music and dance. They are forward-moving in time duration, and rhythm is the impulse behind the word, the tone, the movement. But, here again the symmetry of the past contrasts with the oblique, asymmetrical style of the moderns. The revolt in poetry against Romanticism has brought new metric manifestations that avoid the evenly recurring accents of the Victorian poets, especially the 4/4 tetrameter:

> I hate to learn the ebb of time
> From yon dull steeple's drowsy chime.
> > Sir Walter Scott

However, the metric construction of poetry being based upon the accented and unaccented parts of a word phrase, and not upon a scientific division of time-values, does not share a parallelism with dance as complete as that of music. Therefore, new rhythmic devices in the dance can be compared more closely with those in music.

Musically speaking the term "rhythm" is indeed a multiple one. Besides standing for the regular pulsing of the metric units, it is also accepted as the division of a composition into sentences, phrases, and sections, as marked off by cadences — what A. Eaglefield Hull (Modern Harmony) terms "musical rhyming." Actually rhythm is time, pace and meter rolled into one, but in practice is often used to mean any one of them singly. The meaning here shall be the common version of rhythm; the systematic grouping of pulses; the metric distribution within the measure or phrase.

During the classic and romantic periods practically all music was written in even, pedestrian rhythms; either in 2, 4, and 8, or 3, 6, and 9. As modern art was initially a drive for more freedom, modern composers soon claimed the right to experiment with less inelastic notations. Cyril Scott, in The Philosophy of Modernism, protests "Is it in any sense a pointless query to ask why we should be limited to that regularity, that unvarying three beats or four beats or six beats in a bar, when a much greater variety... could be gained by a constantly varying rhythm or no definite rhythm at all? Surely it is no argument to say that, because for five hundred years a thing has existed in this or that form, therefore it cannot be changed." Most modern composers not only write whole compositions in 5/4 or 7/4 but vary the rhythm from measure to measure. This is a significant practice in music evolution, and has also been very significant in the changing dance.

In his book New Musical Resources, Henry Cowell points out "... how extremely primary the older conception of meter is, in which the same meter is expected to remain unchanged for an entire composition. If in lieu of a melody the same note were to be repeated for an entire work, it would be considered absurd; yet this endless repetition is just what is expected in meter, in which hundreds of the same metrical units, such as measures of 3/4, etc. follow one another without change."

The experimentation away from rhythmic regularity was not only a desire for greater rhythmic freedom and variety; basically it was really a desire for greater fitness to contemporary life, a way toward a new realism, a truth in rhythmic action. It is this view of experimentation in musical rhythms that links it so closely to the contemporary dance's urge toward an honest employment of action-rhythms; rhythms which are based on physiological fact; a true and new realism arising from action not attitude.

Heretofore, composers, when wishing to portray something vague, restless, unbalanced, mysterious, distorted, etc., etc., achieved their ends mostly by the establishment of a tonal mood or atmosphere — the very backbone of Romanticism. The present-day composer is motivated by a greater degree of rhythmic reality. He may feel the dramatic necessity to bring out a mood, but he attains his reality more completely through the use of uneven pulses. The use of uneven action rhythms has enabled the modern dancer to project more honestly many of the conditions of contemporary life. "One of the earmarks of the restlessness of our age is shown in our rhythmic groupings." (Marion Bauer, Twentieth Century Music.)

The unsymmetrical rhythm produced by quintuple time (5/4 or 5/8) and less frequently by 7/4 or 7/8 time, enticed the first modern composers to experiment with them. The five rhythm is usually found in music with an accent on the first count and a secondary one on the third or fourth beat: 12345 or 12345. In dance it is most effective when a segment of 3 counts is juxtaposed to a segment of 2: 123 45 │ 123 45. The ratio of 3 to 2 produces a sharper sense of rhythmic distortion than a ratio of 4 to 2 or 3 to 1. A five rhythm is really a shortened six, and it is the unexpected intrusion of the next following 1 that produces the desired rhythmic jolt. It is an interesting experiment to take a melody or movement that has been constructed in a 5/8 or 5/4 and play or dance it in a 6/8 or 6/4 time. The resultant flatness is inescapable. However, there are many compositions in quintuple time that not only do not seem unnatural, but produce music and movement of swing and ease. In such situations it is employed for greater flexibility. There are fives with no more distortions to them than a five-point star. In Martha Graham's "Hymn to the Virgin" (from Primitive Mysteries, Louis Horst, composer) there are several sections in 5/8 time that do not break the lyric flow of the composition. "Silent Night," played with five counts to a measure instead of the traditional six gives a slightly unbalanced quality to the familiar tune which is interesting but not disturbing. Actually, it is often sung with some of the measures in five time by amateurs who unknowingly fail to wait the full six counts.

Another innovation has been effected by the use of a single beat bar: a time signature of 1/4. The Greeks called this the "monometer." Here the idea of accented and unaccented beats must be firmly put aside. The rhythmic character of each count is to be equally strong 1-1-1, and not 1-2, 1-2, or 1-2-3-4. This rhythm is especially adaptable in dance for single strong movements, whether repeated or not.

Rhythmic developments have by no means ceased with the 1, 5, and 7. Pioneers such as Schoenberg, Berg, Varèse, Cowell, Ives and their disciples, have been and are employing rhythmic devices of such intricate complexity as almost to defy human performance. For a clear exposition of intricate rhythmic possibilities there is nothing better than the section on "Rhythm" in Henry Cowell's New Musical Resources.

The bulk of modern music and dance composition is still fashioned in the even rhythms. Biological forms are for the most part symmetrical (two feet, two shoulders, two ears) and our feeling of comfort in symmetry is very deep. If what were originally called "oblique rhythms" were used always, their effect as departures from the norm would wear out and the result would be as monotonous as even rhythms have become.

DANCE STUDY IN ASYMMETRICAL RHYTHM

The contemporary dancer will sense that as in music, strange rhythms, even with conservative harmony, provide any composition with a translation into modernity. So in dance a use of free metric units will give an otherwise conservatively constructed piece a contemporary significance. Practice in the actual use of asymmetrical counts can give the student a new understanding and sympathy for the uneven rhythms of all the modern arts. It is directly illustrative of the distractions and interruptions prevalent in Twentieth Century life.

Movement to a 5/4 is uneven, oblique, unstable. It may be an appropriate form for comment on the familiar frantic, many-directed existence of people today: the housewife, the college student, a Madison Avenue flannel suit.

In the theatre, actors know that if they come on stage with a walk which is timed to uneven rhythm, the audience will immediately sense that some emotional disturbance has entered into the plot.

The feel of the asymmetrical rhythm must be within the body. Care should be taken, for instance, if a 5/4 is used, not to count 1,2,3,4,5 - 1,2,3,4,5. It should be felt as 1,2,3,4,5,1, so that the 1 breaks into give a strong off-beat effect. Also, as the asymmetrical rhythm is developed into a dance composition, care should be taken that its feeling of unbalance is not destroyed by gestures which create a too symmetrical design in space.

Danse de la Brouette
(La Femme et le Danseur)

Vivace

Erik Satie

Texture

The harmonic element in music was a comparatively late addition. Until medieval days, as far as we know, all music was played or sung in unison. As early as the Ninth Century the device developed of singing open fifths in parallel motion — a form known as organum. When in the Fourteenth Century two modal melodies, and then three, were sung at the same time, a modal counterpoint had developed. It was the simultaneous meeting of these three lines that produced the new element, harmony. Here was a new richness or body between the melody and the fundamental rhythm. But during the Renaissance this modal counterpoint was discarded. The diatonic scales: major (Ionian), minor (Aeolian) gradually took the place of the several old modes, and homophonic composition became the practice. By the time the Romantic age reached its full power nearly all music was homophonic — that is textural, non-linear, and built on harmonic chords. The great writers of this style felt a strong pull toward consonance; rules of harmony demanded that all dissonant chords be resolved.

The harmonic texture in the writings of the moderns is so different from that of the Nineteenth Century that the consideration of the musical element harmony provides another easy way of "understanding by contrast." This is especially true for the layman, who always seems firmly convinced that all classic and romantic music is "consonant," and that all modern music is just as surely "dissonant" and cacophonous. Such a generalization is only partially correct. All classic composers have used dissonance, but the harmonic concepts of the classic and romantic writers which compelled them to have each dissonance resolve into a consonance lent it a sort of "happy ending" philosophy. The moderns, in their need for greater freedom and desire for a more realistic philosophy, refused to be bound by the dictum of "resolution into a consonance," and so introduced a new "edge," a "bite," to the quality of their music by their handling of dissonance without resolution.

Dissonances.

Claude Debussy asked, "Why must I resolve every dissonance? Why can I not go directly from one dissonance to another?" This he did, defying the academicians. He, together with all other impressionist composers, used dissonances freely, even for final points of rest. As with other aesthetic revolutions, we have become so accustomed to this new tonal texture that today the music of the Impressionists seems quite as gentle to our ears as any "sweet concourse of sound." For "dissonance" is not "discord," and should not be confounded with it. It is not the interjecting of wrong notes into an otherwise consonant pattern, but a new tonal approach.

In Twentieth Century Music, Marion Bauer writes, "Dissonance is the point of departure for twentieth century harmony. Where our musical forefathers built on consonance, we study the affinities and repulsions of dissonant combinations. We are more interested in harmonic progressions than in resolutions, because progression implies a fluidic or dynamic state where resolution is immobile or static." There is in dissonance a tension, a state of becoming, a pull toward movement not found in the finality of consonance. The usefulness of such a music to the art of action, which is dance, is obvious. The immobile nature of consonance is further dwelt on by Arnold Schoenberg, who stated "... it is likely that for a time at least consonant chords will have to disappear not for physical reasons, but for reasons of economy. Consonant chords tend to occupy an excessive amount of room."

Other arts experienced the same development. As in music the vibrant and luminous dissonances of the impressionist composers led on to the tonal shocks of a Stravinsky, so in painting, the now seemingly transparent "optical mixture" of the impressionist painters opened the way to the color shocks of a Matisse.

There should be no question of the analogy of this harmonic texture in dance movement. Casella says that harmony is the physical element in music. And that is exactly what it is in dance: that inner physical, muscular consciousness which colors movement and gives it its particular quality. The modern dance turned away from the consonant platitudes and attitudes of the romantic dance and developed its own new speech based on the tensions, realistic expressionism, and inner significance of contemporary life and thought. Following in the steps of the modern painter and the modern composer, the modern dancer has infused movement with that vibrant restless texture and that intense inner concentration typical of our psychologically oriented age.

Untitled Duet — Paul Taylor   Photograph by Louis A. Stevenson Jr.

Although rhythm is probably the most primitive element in dance and music (the drums, the clapping, familiar in primitive societies) and experiments with its wider freedoms are an important feature of the modern dance, dissonance and strange space design are the very core of the new dance. These new versions of the elements line, rhythm and texture have become a philosophy of movement, as natural to it as a new skin. The student must throw off hampering preconceived notions of what dance movement should be and come to feel deeply the expressiveness of dissonance and strange space design in the dance of his own living world.

DANCE STUDY IN DISSONANCE

Experimentation and practice in strongly dissonant movement will widen the student's resources and provide him with a new coloring, vivid and strong, to apply to any of the subsequent dance forms studied.

This is not grotesque movement. It is a state of physical being throughout the body — a complete physical awareness which furnishes the dance with a new texture: tense, full of potential action, one part pulling against another.

To be effective, there is needed here a rather high degree of technique. Tension cannot be indicated, it must be actual. At this point, perhaps, it should be emphasized that the inexperienced dancer will not be more effective by attempting movements beyond his control, but less so. Of course, there must be a continuous effort to expand those limits of control, but as soon as the limits are exceeded sharpness and clarity are gone and nothing much is communicated.

Fluid, sequential or soft movements are not to be forgotten, but, in this study, there should be a conscious search for the physical sensation, deep in the muscles, for the texture which speaks of a tension characteristic of the modern world.

Diſſonanzen

Lothar Windsperger

Ziemlich rasch, aufgeregt (Allegro agitato)

Backgrounds or Sources

Primitivism

In his book Expressionism in Art Sheldon Cheney writes:
"The moderns, indeed, go to man's past reverently. They
recognize the life of the ages as soil from which contemporary
art takes nourishment." The error of ignoring tradition is
as great as succumbing to it. Modern artists inevitably turn
back to ancient cultures, and in all fields find especial inspiration in the Primitive, the Archaic, and the Medieval. The
Classic and the Renaissance (which was a rebirth of the Greek
ideal of proportion and symmetry) have been largely ignored
by contemporary artists searching for vital new directions.

Modern art was born as a violent reaction against four centuries of Renaissance domination. Artists rebelling against
the overblown superficiality of the late Romantic age demanded
solid ground from which they could begin at the beginning to
formulate their ideas. Primitive means the beginning. So it
was the naïve but powerful simplicity of primitive people that
provided the desired vigor and directness that the art pioneers
needed. They went back into man's remote past in order to
go forward. Thus primitive art has been by far the strongest
distinguishing influence for all the moderns.

The Nineteenth Century Romantics had been producing music
which cascaded in pearly notes and rains of octaves. Literature was over-borne with purple adjectives and flowery prose
and with sentimentality:

I never nursed a dear gazelle
To glad me with its soft black eye,
But when it grew to know me well
And love me, it was sure to die.   Thomas Moore

Architectural facades were broken out in a rash of windows,
pinnacles, and scroll work. Dancers aspired to skim and
spin like heavenly puff-balls. So at the end of the last century
it was evident that the old had to be abandoned and a new beginning made. "The surface soil had become exhausted. It
had to be turned deeply and completely to produce anything
young in vigor or sap." (James Johnson Sweeney, Plastic
Redirections in 20th Century Painting)

The moderns repudiated romantic formulae with violence.
Bluntness was exalted, and the artist set out to demolish the
existing prejudices about beauty and ugliness. Paint went onto canvas straight from the tube; music became more percussive; the dancer moved with a conscious awkwardness;
writing grew more terse, more abrupt. The artist had recov-
ered a primitive attitude. Robert J. Goldwater in his analysis,
Primitivism in Modern Painting, describes the various directions in which this back-to-the-beginning attitude has led
different creative artists: Klee is a "child primitive," Gauguin
is a "romantic" primitive, the German Expressionists "emotional," Picasso and Modigliani "intellectual," Rousseau and
the Surrealists "subconscious," and so forth. All are primi-
tivistic. In other words primitive art is evident as a strong
quality in every contemporary style.

Those early pioneers felt that by first going back to the less
sophisticated point of view of the primitive they could then go
forward to the discovery of a way of painting a poetic reality
instead of imitating a visual one. And so we find Paul Klee
crying out, "I want to be as though new-born. . .knowing no
pictures, entirely without impulses, almost in an original

Grande Danseuse - 1907 — Pablo Picasso
Collection of Walter P. Chrysler, Jr.

Ancestor Figure — Gaboon, Africa
Courtesy, Chicago Natural History
Museum

Primitive Canticles — Martha Graham   Photograph by Barbara Morgan

state." Kandinsky has described the artist as being throughout his life similar to children, and says that as children, he
can attain the inner harmony of things more easily than other
men. The various eager searches for fundamental laws and

a fresh point of view led the experimenters to African Negro sculpture, archaic painting, children's drawings, dream imagery and the intimate patterns of nature.

The old poetry, which had been noble, sweet, regular and sonorous, gave way to disturbingly new arrangements of words and even invention of words. Poets felt need for dissonance and discord to kill the saccharine taste of romantic harmony. They murdered form, syntax, the sentence, definitions and logic. The "back to the primitive" urge brought plainer language, a subject matter which shunned the heroic but picked up minutiae of daily experience, simple and shorter verse forms, and sometimes a shock-making abruptness and frankness. For instance, compare Tennyson's "Ode on the Death of the Duke of Wellington" to the unadorned thrust of W. H. Auden's "Epitaph on a Tyrant":

> Perfection, of a kind, was what he was after,
> And the poetry he invented was easy to understand;
> He knew human folly like the back of his hand,
> And was greatly interested in armies and fleets;
> When he laughed, respectable senators burst with laughter,
> And when he cried the little children died in the streets.

It is extreme in Samuel Beckett's work where his preoccupation with the barest elements of the physical existence of man — his breathing, heart beats, ambulation — bring his writing as close to a primordial animal basis as is possible through language.

Late Nineteenth Century sculptors, too, when coming in contact with figures from Africa, were stimulated by the oneness and harmony that they found existed between the primitive artisan and the materials he worked with. The power which lies in the way the primitive interrelates the parts of his whole figure, and the abridgment to meaning he achieves through the broad use of symbols, are points of strength emulated by all contemporary sculptors.

Contemporary art and primitive art have a relationship deeper than surface resemblances. Modern man is not an aborigine, and the productions of adults are not the same as those of children. A truly primitive approach would be an affectation today. The resemblances lie in the adaptation by the modern of the single-minded intensity of emotion which is the starting place of the primitive, and of his scrupulous sensibility to fundamentals of materials and the interplay of abstract forms. The so-called naïveté of Matisse is derived from the nature of his vision. Actually, his work is based upon a skill of disciplined sophistication. Stravinsky's barbaric violences become Twentieth Century orchestral comment in his <u>Rites of Spring</u>. The vivid qualities of primitive art are used, not in the manner of a documentation, but are incorporated in a new aesthetic. Let us review these qualities.

This art is functional. Its distortion is devised, not to satisfy any aesthetic laws, but to make it effective — in primitive society toward a magic end. The primitive did not create works of art, but magic weapons. The materials, as well as the shapes of movements he used, bore magic properties. The present-day artist again uses distortion functionally. The element of magic, the supernatural, the beyond-comprehension, brings with it a quality of awe, wonder, and strangeness — the feeling of something coming out of the unknown. Vision through the unjaded eye of a child is the conscious or unconscious aim of the primitivist. This does not mean that it is technically inadequate, only that, as Clive Bell puts it, "technical swagger is stripped away." The primitive expression is often one of violence and always of striking vitality. It is above all simple and direct. "Its primary concern is with the elemental, and its simplicity comes from direct and strong feeling, which is a very different thing from that fashionable simplicity for-its-own-sake which is emptiness." (Henry Moore). Nietzsche has said that "the primitive mind is a one-track mind." The simple direct route is often one of asymmetry. Primitivism has released us from the tyranny of

Reclining Figure — Henry Moore
Courtesy, Room of Contemporary Art, Albright Art Gallery, Buffalo, New York

symmetry; the question followed by the answer in music, the right-hand movement to balance the left in dance. The way of the primitive is repetition rather than sequence.

Finally, the primitivists are animated by a search for something formal. They are not concerned with naturalistic imitation. They use symbols as the equivalents of the natural, and devise conventionalizations (the faces of Modigliani, the stick figures of Klee). In primitive times men did not hope to understand the mysteries of physical forces, so the half-truths of symbols represented for them the forefront of their understanding of life. Nowadays we again turn to dependence on symbols, but this time not because they represent the unknown to us as they did for the primitive, but because they evoke emotional, instinctive ways of understanding. These conventionalizations lead the modern artist to simplicity and unity.

For the dance student, and especially the apprentice choreographer, a conscious assimilation of the primitive's directness — an ability to derive dance movement from life experience rather than from a sort of decorative habit — is of first importance. It is well for him not only to examine the art of primitive cultures and study its appearance in all the arts of today, but for him to experience its qualities through short compositions in the pure primitive style. The following exercises will help him absorb into his muscular repertory the movements and moods which carry the attributes of primitivism just described. By much conscious use of the style he will be able to call upon it instinctively when it is appropriate to his ideas. He will have at his disposal the wonderfully expressive language learned from primitive art — the awkwardness, the bluntness, the naïveté, the spontaneity, the vitality and strength.

In a primitive dance study the gestures are simple and direct like a child's or an animal's. The movement is sparse and unelaborated like the primitive's speech (a Southwest Indian, responding to the fiery splendor of a setting sun, described it with only one word, "Sunset!"). There is a distortion which reflects the fear and smallness of man in face of all nature. The movement is asymmetrical. Ordered balance in design developed with Classicism and Romanticism. All the dance mood is closely related to magic and awe and has the stillness and fullness of wonder. It is a ritual of propitiation, of mysterious gods in the earth and sky. It echoes signs, omens, magic talismen, fetishes, hieratic ceremony, prescribed rites.

The strangeness of this language has nothing to do with exoticism (even though only a few years ago the one card in the New York Public Library filed under "Primitive" was annotated "see Exotic"). A primitive dance is not produced by portraying "The End of the Trail" or the gyrations of a monster hanging by its tail. The primitive movement partakes of the "divine awkwardness" of which Martha Graham speaks. It is always expressive of a "first seeing," a "first feeling," a "first experience."

The dancer must come to a deep understanding of the texture of this important mode by composing dance studies in two different types of primitivism. The gods of simple peoples are magic figures: denizens of either the earth or the air. Two suggested choreographic exercises will help the student to assimilate variations of the style. The first is the Earth Primitive, the second the Air Primitive.

EARTH PRIMITIVE DANCE STUDY

For an Earth Primitive study, movement can be experimented with which will suggest the mysterious powers that abide in the earth. Such a dance study invokes the mood and creates the texture of the primitive in his relation to the world beneath him.

The dancer is alertly sensitive to the feel of the earth under his feet. It is the genesis and grave of all living things — the source and the finale. The movements are in the lower areas and oriented to the floor. They can be clumsy and animalistic. They can be brutal and threatening. They can project the lyricism of wonder, or the tenderness of the giver of life. They may have a drum-like percussiveness. But always they are simple and meagerly articulated; lean and taut. All movements seem to receive their vitality from the earth and explore the areas of that direct relationship between man and the ground he emerges from.

The primitive walk (feet straight or turned in) might be the primal discovery that a human being can walk — every step an adventure, an exploration. "Come down into the earth with your heels!" Martha Graham tells her pupils. "Walk as if for the first time."

Any gestures that are fluid, smooth, or slick are avoided; everything kept down to a simple bareness. In the primitive society of our own Southwest Indian the body expresses stoicism — is held rather like a totem pole, with ankles and wrists not too articulated. It moves with an evidence of limited vocabulary; for instance, the hand in one piece with the arm, or the whole body turned to the point of attention. The subject

<u>Emperor Jones</u> — Danced and choreographed by José Limon
Photograph by Radford Bascome

matter can be drawn out of primal experiences; the mysteries of a planting ceremony, or a burial ritual, or any form of earth worship. Almost any subjective experience can be treated as primal: love, search, fear, discovery, etc.

AIR PRIMITIVE DANCE STUDY

The other primitive study, the Air Primitive, will suggest mysterious powers that abide in the air above the earth. This dance reflects a more sophisticated attitude toward its subject. It arises from a culture with a greater acquaintance and surety in the physical world — is not bound to the simple, most basic mother earth.

The Air Primitive has to do with uncanny airy things; with birds, feathers, witches, fire and fire magic, with omens, apparitions, and enchantments, and with the sun and the wind. Our words "incantation" (in-singing), "invocation" (in-voicing), "inspiration" (in-breathing), all indicate a use of the breath to invoke supernatural powers. The Southwest Indians begin their dance prayers with aspirants such as "hey-ah." Their gods are the Great Spirit (Great Breath) and air borne divinities such as fire gods, the Thunderbird, the Plumed Serpent. In all the tribes feathers are indispensable to ceremonial costumes and to designs. Paul Morand, in his book Indian Air, proposes that all of Europe, except Spain, is earth-minded, while the aboriginal cultures of the Americas are air-minded. In Latin America the air-minded cultures (Spanish and Indian) have been successfully blended. It is with the Indians of Spanish America that this kind of dance finds repeated source.

FOURTEEN BAGATELLES

I.

Béla Bartók
op. 6 no. 1

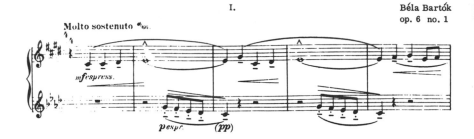

The movements of the Air Primitive must have a focus into the air. They will include anything air-borne, anything that draws the body up from the ground into the space above it: leaps, hops, runs, flutterings, wing movements. There is a more open, transparent quality than in the Earth Primitive. With the increased freedom of a release from the earth, the dancer's body becomes more articulated, a little less clumsy, but it must retain some of the primitive quality of awkwardness and awe which leads to distortion of line.

Suggested subject matter includes fire rituals, rain ceremonies, sacrificial rites, bird auguries, witches' spells, evil spirits, apparitions or exhortation. Among psychological themes hallucination, delusion, etc., can be developed in this air primitive style.

Although almost all modern choreography is primitive to a degree, some fine compositions have been almost completely cast in a primitive mold: Martha Graham's Primitive Mysteries and Primitive Canticles and Deep Song; José Limon's Emperor Jones; Doris Humphrey's With My Red Fires.

Bird Spell — Iris Mabry   Photograph by Louise Dahl-Wolfe

CANTS MÁGICS

No. 2

Obscur

Federico Mompou

Etruscan Figure Woman Dancing
Courtesy, Museum of Fine Arts, Boston, Mass.

The Archaic

The earliest art expressions, answering to our description of "the Primitive" in the previous section, are almost purely functional; their forms determined by the practical considerations of work, war, or religion. The archaic period, growing very gradually out of the primitive, gives birth to something new — aesthetic consciousness. The tribal artisan or dancer who petitioned the gods in primitive ritual becomes the artist breaking through the ritual, conscious of formal beauty for the first time. He is completely absorbed in the newly discovered aesthetic ideal, and this absorption makes for an intensity and an awareness of detail, of color, line, texture and design. A creative passion supercedes his emotion as a mere worshipper. The craftsman who fashioned forms for service evolves into the artist who creates them because they are beautiful.

The sculptured figures of the great archaic periods of Greek, Cretan and Etruscan cultures are stark, planal, and powerful. They were born in the games stadium and of the gymnastic cult of a virile people who worshipped the agile and the strong, but were at the same time guided by a new-born reverence for reason. It is true that there are some ancient peoples (the Egyptians and Babylonians) who became so completely obsessed by a formal architectural conception in their works of art, that they were led to a dryness of abstraction like the one that threatens some modern artists. But typically the archaic style is one of a vigorously growing culture, one of great strength and forceful directness.

All the arts express the same tautness and starkness: the clean, simple early Greek temples, the stripped, abstracted Etruscan statues, the arranged, uncluttered decoration on early vases. The modal music of that time, too, so favored by some modern composers, has a sort of tautness which arises from its asymmetric intervals.

In the Nineteenth Century, when art was excessively naturalistic, primitive art was given no consideration at all, and the archaic arts were regarded as naïvely unsuccessful attempts by early peoples to achieve the then current romantic standards of realism. Now we are able to see that archaic distortions were deliberate — were consistently devised by those artists in order to attain the formal harmony and unity which was their ideal of beauty.

Above all, the archaic gives a strong feeling of design. Each part of the composition must relate to every other part even to the smallest detail. There is an intense absorption in balance and arrangement instead of verisimilitude. The motion in the figures seems to be arrested in order to give a poised and restrained sense of beauty for its own sake. A strict discipline and an impersonal concise attitude on the part of the artist is necessary in order to arrive at the desired perfection of relationship between the elements in the design. His discipline denies him the suppleness of three dimensions. With a combination of mind and eye, he reduces his forms to planes, selecting what is essential and permanent and omitting the irrelevant. It is in this abridgment, this abstraction, that the contemporary artist feels very close to the archaic.

The whole art expression of the Twentieth Century has been characterized by a return to archaism — to art as a vital element in itself, not merely as reflection of practical life. The rhythms of Cezanne's architectonic arrangement of planes is perhaps the archetype. We feel the perfect organization and relationship of all parts in his pictures, built up between the various flattened surfaces — a tension of arrested movement that is typical of archaism. All modern painters

Women on Balcony — Massimo Campigli
Courtesy, World House Galleries, New York

Leap — Merce Cunningham   Photograph by Gerda Peterich

put paint on canvas in formally organized designs of lines and planes. There is no "background" like the comparatively relaxed and non-participating area around a Rembrandt portrait. The dancer, too, meticulously arranges his movement in space with that same disciplined formality, feeling the stress of these interrelationships appropriate to the stress of contemporary life.

The archaic artist displays constant concern with the materials he is working with. The modern artist repeats the archiac attitude in his complete absorption with his materials: the painter is absorbed with putting paint on canvas, the sculptor with shaping his formal design in space, the composer with the projection of sonorities, and the dancer with movement.

A complete physical awareness is basic to both the archaic style and the modern dance. Every modern dancer is archaic in his unceasing consciousness of his whole body and its intense potential for movement even when at rest. This body consciousness is not just one of line, but of organization so that action in any part of the body is felt in every other part. Each detail, even to ear or fingertip, has an awareness of participation in each action. This means that the design of the whole body in space has been considered in order to realize _formal_ unity.

DANCE STUDY IN THE ARCHAIC

Dance studies in the strict discipline of movement in archaic style train the body to exactitude, and the dancer to an alert awareness of his instrument in space. The planal relationship to the audience — the visual aspect of the movement, not the emotional texture — is of primary consideration.

This study is one simply of movement experience and need not have a subject matter. It is simple and architectural.

In this style of dance, the distortion necessary to force the human body into a two-dimensional design creates a tension which gives the composition great strength. Sensualism is replaced by a rigid formality, a scrupulous discipline. At the same time the dance is strikingly alive. The control, the understatement, the tautness should give it a quality of excitement completely unsentimental. The design is angular by nature of its two-dimensional directness (as in the familiar pattern of ancient Egyptian art). Tension pulls the curve out of the line as the curve has been pulled out of a stretched rope. Formality is always a little rigid — even in social relationships.

Archaism is life arrested in attitudes that breathe at the same time a potential of movement (like a sequence of moving picture stills) attitudes connected one with another, designs changing in time but each one sustained through into the next. The first dance composition of our time which was conspicuously archaic in feeling was Nijinsky's L'Apres-Midi d'un Faune, so revolutionary in 1912 when it was new.

It should be remembered that in planal design every element is equally important. Nothing is casual. The mood must be sustained with the intensity of a slow-motion picture; in fact, the first studies should be done in a tempo so slow that the illusion of slow-motion photography will result.

GNOSSIENNE
(1890)

ERIK SATIE

Nº 2

Avec étonnement

PIANO

Ne sortez pas

Dans une grande bonté

Medievalism

The classic burgeoning of the Golden Age of Greece represented a period when the sure formula of the Golden Mean satisfied everyone, and art was a complete and perfect expression of its time. Subsequently, this Greek classicism, adopted by the materialistic society of the Romans, became mundane without the genius of its founders, and degenerated finally into the realism of the late Roman Empire.

The succeeding Christian era, and the move of the capital of the Empire from Rome to Byzantium in 322 A.D., injected a new vigor into all the art expression of that civilized world. With the zeal of westward-spreading Christianity, this new vigor was carried back through Europe and nourished what we now call typical medieval art. Medieval culture persisted with little variation until, after a thousand years, the aesthetic upheaval of the Renaissance superceded it in Western Europe. Although the Twentieth Century artist finds little that is creatively stimulating in classic and renaissance art, the medieval style of expression may reveal much that is sympathetic and provocative to him.

The Catholic Church, great unifying force in these centuries, gave shape and substance to the arts of the middle ages. It met almost every human need — social, moral, and intellectual — and so, strongly affected the inner mind of the times. Human ideals all found their seat in Heaven. Earthly

Martyrdom of Saint Juliet — Spanish circa 1100
Reproduced from SPAIN, Romanesque Painting, Volume VII of the UNESCO World Art Series, Courtesy of New York Graphic Society, Greenwich, Connecticut

experiences were profane. The devil was termed "Prince of this Earth." For the individual the Christian philosophy held ideals of meekness, self abnegation, denial of physical satisfactions, disavowal of bodily appetites. These were to be foregone in this life for the promise of a sure reward in a life after death. It was an age in which monastic orders were restricted by silence, fasting and celibacy, of ascetic withdrawal. To continue successfully in these trying and unnatural habits of living it was necessary constantly to practice penitence, to mortify the flesh to save the soul. The agony of martyrdom was sought as a way to heaven. The evidence of superstitious beliefs and miraculous happenings is suffused through every record of medieval life and thought. Because the creed of the church emphasized the supernatural powers of heaven, natural laws were of small importance. Throughout the whole range of paintings, mosaics, sculpture, tapestries, the physical laws of gravity are denied and the figures seem out of balance, contorted, deformed, pale and unearthly. Sometimes footless, they seem to hang in the air. There is a strange disregard of any perspective; backgrounds are reduced, and groups of figures appear to be piled one upon another. The composition is as irregular as the battlements of a medieval castle.

The strongest element of design in all the medieval arts is that of parallelism. The pull and stress of opposition, as in the pagan Archaic, connotes strength, but conversely, parallelism when applied to the Christian figure is illustrative of the meek acceptance of earthly trials which is the core of the philosophy of the middle ages. The soaring lines of the ecclesiastical architecture are parallel, and the designs in the paintings of that time seem to echo in unopposing submission the precepts of the church.

Parallelism is a feature of the ecclesiastic music, organum: an invention of medieval times. Instead of the unison singing

Angel of Annunciation — Harald Kreutzberg
Drawing by Nicolai Remisoff

of the Gregorian Chant, organum combines melodic parts in
a simultaneous progression of voices in parallel fifths. All
voices lead in the same direction. The rhythm established
by the irregularity of the word phrasing of the liturgy, creates
a resultant quality of distorted rhythmic unbalance. When,
in due course, the rational-minded Renaissance supplanted
the Medieval, it ran full tilt against irregular rhythm, consecutive fifths and vocal progression, and it banned these
practices as weakness. Only with the growth of the modern
musical writing has organum again become an important design for composition.

The intentional lack of the superficially romantic in medieval
art, its simplicity, distortion, irregularity and pale parallelism are attributes akin to the new artistic language of the
modern creative artist in every field, and have been adapted
to contemporary themes by all the leading choreographers.

Familiarity with movement in the mood
and style of the period just described
adds a distinctive language of expressiveness to the store of the dancer.
Basically this is distinguished by its
irregularity of rhythm and its parallelism. Parallelism in dance demands
that the various parts of the body go in
the same direction (like the voices of the
organum music): two hands, two shoulders,
two feet, two knees, and head and torso
all following the directed design.

In the study of medieval art we find a division into a religious
style and a secular style. While both are built on the same
principles, these principles are used in such different ways
that it is advisable to describe each of them. Both will be
related to parallelism and irregularity of rhythm,

RELIGIOUS MEDIEVAL DANCE STUDY

The first style is based on religious ecstacy. It is weak with a weakness born of meekness and a paleness born of self-denial. Dance movement based on the parallel designs of medieval religious art is attenuated or twisted out of natural postures to a point of torture. It is apt to be performed in a very limited area; for the most part moving from one parallel design to another without covering much floor space. Besides the anguished deformity, the manner is one of unrealness, of the miraculous. It decries the human and the worldly, defies gravity and normal earthly forces and seems

Les Stigmates de S! François. Mihi autem

Paul de Maleingreau

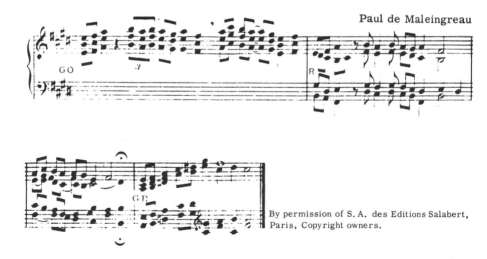

to be supported only by faith. The dance will repeat the elongated, reaching, contorted art of those times. The conception of medieval man suffering under an inner, self-inflicted pain is plainly analogous to many of our familiar modern psychological ideas of emotional conflicts and complexes, and the style is consequently one which is appropriate to this subject matter.

Dances about self-inflicted penance, fasting, flagellation, denial of the world suggest themselves; or in psychological terminology: guilt complexes, withdrawals, etc. Lives of medieval saints and martyrs can be examined for subject matter for a religious medieval dance study — the hair shirt, the straw pallet. It must not be forgotten that although a religious medieval dance is always religious, a religious dance is not always medieval. There should be no confusion with the Renaissance portrayal of religious subjects. Mixed and uneven rhythm give the needed uneven, asymmetrical, oblique character to the dance design.

Die Minnesänger 1221-24   German Manuscript

SECULAR MEDIEVAL DANCE STUDY

The secular style is more mundane than the preceding one,
so that the twisted, the tortured are not used so intensively.
Applied to the dance it produces a movement strange to the

Graue Kraft von Toggenburg.

eye as the old English words of Chaucer are strange to the ear:

> Whan that Aprille with his showres sote
> The droghte of Marche hath perced to the rote...

Even the tempo and texture of life outside the church shared in an attitude which grew out of ecclesiastical denial of the significance of the earthly life. Our knowledge of life in Western Europe in medieval times and of the way people acted and thought is limited by what we can imply from pictures and writings, stories and building styles. A study of these sources is the best way to become familiar with the genre. Chaucer's <u>Canterbury Tales</u>, for instance, make vivid various kinds of people in England of the Fourteenth Century; the Bayeux Tapestry, which chronicles the Norman Conquest, is a wonderfully rich source to consult for information about daily doings and costumes of everyday life of the Twelfth Century. <u>The Golden Book</u> — designed as home entertainment for people of that day — presents a series of pictures depicting activities appropriate to each month of the year. The miraculous feats of acrobats and jugglers and the tales of troubadours, minstrels, trouvères, took the place in that day of the mass of periodicals, books and moving pictures that amuse us. Illustrations, twisted or contorted, of all these entertainments abound in the records of the times. The words of the old Chansons and Pastorals tell of the daily life in castle and cottage, of love, of trials of strength, and of contests of skill. Mythical creatures belong to this lore too: the roc, the unicorn, dragons, gargoyles, witches and fairies. All offer rich material for dance studies in the style.

La Dame à la Licorne — Helen McGehee
Photograph by Raymond Whyte

Authentic historical figures need not be portrayed, but themes selected should always be permeated with the qualities of the fantastic, the quaint, the unbelievable, and done with perkiness, piquancy, fragility, and a kind of constriction. There may be garden scenes, scenes of grotesque humor, pastorals, coquetries, plaints of love — light themes. There is never anything signifying robustness or earthiness — no sweeping gestures, but movements that are small and repressed; always asymmetrical, irregular, parallel, without the pull of opposition.

CHANSON DU PÊCHEUR

Charles Koechlin

Mr. Horst Criticizes Dance Studies in the RELIGIOUS MEDIEVAL

This is just another channel of strange, distorted parallel movement.
You must get some sense of ecstacy to the point of distortion.

Taut, twisted, weak — but a strong weakness.

Everything goes one way — hip, shoulders, head.

Face front!
Look up!
Leg that goes up should be the one in the direction of movement, not the opposite.

Head looks straight forward. If it drops forward it becomes romantic.
Get a tortured, two dimensional quality.

Don't "lift" the leg — let the hip pull it up!
Don't let your head drop back.

I know it hurts! But these things are supposed to represent pain and suffering.

It's not easy.

Denial — hair shirts — bare boards to sleep on — being a martyr.

You get it sometimes and then lose it. Go down in a "miraculous" way — this is
a miraculous age — deny gravitation.

Don't be "balanced" — just a dancer on the floor.

You don't believe in the Lord — maybe you're in the wrong religion.

It's difficult — but it's good for you. You must find your balance. You're
trying, but try more — a little more tautness and tenseness — "feel it" —
the suffering and the ecstacy. The more they suffered the nobler they were —

Now — who else?

The Immediacies of Modern Life

Introspection, Expressionism

Freud's revelations concerning the subconscious have seeped into every corner and level of society. Inaccurate as the layman's knowledge of the subject may be, we all have a "psychological approach" to daily experience. Freudian explanations of the intricate interdependence of man's impulsive and rational being are now accepted guides to understanding human conduct and have taken the place of traditional precepts that have lost prestige. The old, moralistic judgments "he is a good boy," "he is a bad boy," have been replaced by complex diagnostic studies of the causes and type of this boy's "maladjustment." We see present theories about inter-personal relationships affecting business, education, domestic life, friendships, and most conspicuously, artistic expression.

Because the Freudian view of man has greatly emphasized the uniqueness of each individual, the point of view of each man is accepted "as if" exclusively and individually his own. It is unique in the sense of a self-conscious subjective individualism which takes the place of the former naturalism of Jean Jacques Rousseau. And so the work of each artist, too, is expected to be unique in form and content because it is produced by his unique personality. "Expressionism," like the fiercely personal painting of Van Gogh, has succeeded "Impressionism." The complex inner world of the emotions which depth psychology has disclosed, suggests a new realm for the artists' inspiration and consideration, and new areas and new definitions of beauty. In the Nineteenth Century prettiness and beauty were woefully synonymous. The arts were so

Melancholia — Edvard Munch
Collection of Herbert Mayer   Courtesy, World House Galleries, New York

/ 9 より

artistic! All the arts, but especially dancing, were expected to express happiness and joy, or a romantic sort of sorrow. It was "bad taste" to show one's inner feelings, and certain intimately personal emotional subjects "were not material for art." Art restricted in these ways was of necessity superficial, i.e., concerned with appearances. The present-day artist, impatient with shallowness, adventures into any realm which has to do with human beings and uses anything he discerns there as material for his aesthetic form. The paradoxical (or seemingly irrational) world of the "unconscious" is now an accepted area for exploration in which literature, painting, drama and also dance find their comments and plots.

The first conspicuously analytical approach to art expression appeared in Russia before Freud's discoveries. The introverted Russian character produced the soul-searching music of Scriabin, and the pitiless self-analysis of Dostoievsky, whom Freud called "the first modern psychologist." The plots of Dostoievsky's novels and the plots of Andreyev's dramas depend for their development on the inner emotional struggles of the characters.

The disenchanted cynicism and pessimism which swept the Western world in the Nineteen-Twenties were responsible for an extreme harshness of expression unforgettably powerful in Germany. Painters such as the German, Nolde, or the Norwegian, Munch, reflect a new psychological point of view in intensely personal presentations of their ideas. Strange proportions and juxtapositions discernible in the unconscious are repeated on their canvases. Often today the non-objective painter quite obviously expresses the turmoil of his internal, subjective world with colors and abstract shapes.

The new poetry and fiction display a passionate desire to achieve an expressiveness which is truer than logic and realer than experience. Writers reach the unconscious perceptions of the reader by inducing in him an identification with their own unconscious flux of imagery.

The stream of consciousness technique of writing, used in different degrees to create different effects, tells its story through the flow of imagery — imagery distorted, as we know it to be, by extraneous events and stifled emotions, but relentless in its subjectivity. The form developed, of course, from psychoanalytic revelations of human character. In this kind of writing emotionally driven thought becomes the action. The life of the unconscious (which is fed with sensory images, not the codified data of a culture) is revealed to consciousness and examined apart from the preconceived abstractions of a culture. Sometimes the writer leaves the reader to fill out and complete the projection with his imagination somewhat as Klee does in his sparse painting.

Similarities between writers and painters meet one often. With both, there is a strong emphasis on connotations and the reminiscence of meanings. Sometimes Dylan Thomas resembles the mad Expressionist Van Gogh with his ferocious colors and exploding forms, or the Surrealists with their startling associative suggestions. Thomas's description (note here also the strange asymmetrical rhythm) of a low London dive:

> There were deep green faces, dipped in a sea dye, with painted cockles for mouths and lichenous hair, sealed on the cheeks; red and purple, slate-gray, tide-marked, rat-brown and stickily white-washed, with violet-inked eyes or lips the colour of Stilton; pink chopped, pink lidded, pink as the belly of a new-born monkey. (from Adventures in the Skin Trade)

In the theatre the actor studies the "psychology" of his role, and the playwright builds his plot as the inevitable consequence of psychological tensions between the characters (O'Neill, Arthur Miller, Pirandello). Martha Graham's typical dramatic scene is laid within the mind or heart of a woman faced with an urgency for decision or action, and with the dramatis personae of the group performing as symbols of her complex emotional reactions. Expressionist theatre settings

Stage Setting for Archibald Mac Leish's <u>J.B.</u> — Boris Aronson
Courtesy of Mr. Aronson

are designed to produce an introspective mood, to evoke an almost dream-like quality by their unspecific forms and eerie lighting. In his plays Samuel Beckett takes reality apart and creates a world on the stage in which the scene of action is the human personality and where human traits perform as the dramatis personae.

Musicians have taken the easy outward expanding harmonies of Romanticism and tortured them with dissonance so that they assume a strong personal flavor suggesting Freudian overtones. Even the architect is accused by Behrendt of being "a product mainly of self contemplation," and of getting into a "blind alley of expressionism." Any expressionism is a blind alley when it contains principally a display of personal emotional ecstasy, for then it has become inadequate to the nonsentimental realism of our age.

The person who was queer because he was "just bashful," is now suffering from "a neurosis." Innumerable terms and phrases have taken on a meaning for us unheard of a hundred years ago: "inhibition," "identification," "compulsion," "fixation." Technical psychological jargon has spread through daily talk: "suppressed desire," "defense mechanism," "inferiority complex." The altruistic Romanticism of the preceding period was outgoing, centrifugal. Today's egoistic focus of interest is turned inward to individual idiosyncracies — centripetal. The romantic composer or poet of the last century wrote "To a Wild Rose," "To Thine Eyes," "To the Skylark." The "interpretative" dancer's piece was directed "to my audience." The present egocentric point of attention often expresses a new kind of Romanticism: "to myself," "to my split personality," "to my alter ego."

Psychological analysis is not only reflected in most dance compositions these days, but is the actual subject matter of introspective works in the repertory of many companies: Tudor's Undertow, Robbin's Facsimile, Graham's Every Soul is a Circus, Sokolow's Rooms, among them.

<u>Traumgestalt</u> — Mary Wigman   Photograph by Charlotte Rudolph, Dresden

DANCE STUDY IN INTROSPECTION

Body movements for a study which will surely create the introspective mood are focused inward to the ego (intro means inward; spective means looking). The inward-turning (introverted) gesture is inevitable from the Freudian emphasis on the prime importance of the individual personality. The dance movement only goes out in order immediately to come in again.

It is impossible for the human body to move in an in-pointing way without some distortion of the normal. This sort of movement distortion was the first that appeared in the modern dance. The early experimenters were intensely introspective in their search for appropriate movement, and were prone to turn in all parts of the body: knees, feet, elbows, hands.

Now we recognize the introverted focus as defining psychological strife. The distortion immediately suggests, in its twisted physical attitudes, a maladjusted mental attitude: an attitude resulting from inabilities, uncertainties and self-induced fears. The movement is not only tortured, but truly clinical in its abnormality. Pulls toward different desires at the same time can be so violently at odds that a "split personality" results. Then the dance may present two qualities at the same time. Or there can be a "transference" from the dancer to a material object: the struggling ego has become so obsessed that emotional qualities are "displaced" to a chair, a wall, etc. Because the psyche in this dance is maladjusted, the dance design, the body lines, must be maladjusted too.

The Desperate Heart — Valerie Bettis   Photograph by Barbara Morgan

The introspective dance study draws upon what was learned in several of the foregoing discussions of styles of movement. It especially relates to the primitive. The psychoanalyst assists the patient to understand his own personality by leading him back to early experiences of his childhood in order to examine the primary impulses deep beneath the veneer of civilization in the realm of the id, ego, and superego. Many of the movements in this genre will, therefore, have the quality of the primitive.

The introspective style of movement may also be reminiscent of the medieval in its parallelism and weakness. A maladjusted and introverted person hesitates to face normal, outside life, and, if compelled, faces it weakly.

When introspective topics and movements were first used for dance, they were thought to be very ugly and completely inappropriate for an art which had been habitually expected to express joy. It still is dangerous material because it can easily lead to the sterility of self-expressionism. Sheldon Cheney has lamented that "Art is made a funnel for belching up from the subconscious." (from Expressionism in Art) This completely subjective language must be used with subtlety and taste or the results will be over-obvious and embarrassing.

Subject matter can be drawn out of experiences and situations familiar to anybody today. Clinical terms which suggest dance ideas are innumerable: self-accusation, frustration, schizophrenia, any kind of fixation, arrested development, case history, and so on. A love dance, in this instance, is an aberration of love, twisted and forbidden. These studies can have the violence of unresolved conflict, or they can portray a quiet of inhibition or melancholia.

PRÉLUDE.

Très lent, contemplatif.
(Sehr langsam, beschaulich.)

Alexander Scriabin, Op. 74. No. 2

Piano.

Mr. Horst Criticizes Dance Studies in INTROSPECTION

Something has to happen to you that makes us feel it.
It should happen in the body before you even start.

Try to get a tighter pattern.

It's time some of you vain babies, who have a "body beautiful"
complex about your dancing, realize that an expressive body is
more beautiful than an inexpressive one. But no, you fight dis-
torting your body — even the least bit. If you won't, you won't,
but your dancing will be shallow, and as empty as the baby stare
some of you are cultivating.

I'm not asking you to tie yourself up like a pretzel or grovel on
the floor, but there must be some distortion if you are portraying
even a slight case of mental maladjustment — a little inferiority
or martyr complex.

You can't drag an analyst's couch out on the stage and tell us
about it. You have to express the mental with your body, so you
distort the movement somewhat to externalize.

You'd better find a way — find some way to express it through
your walk, too. The walk was too healthy. A maladjustment of
your feet — a strange turned-inness.

It was better, and I suppose if I kept you up there for a half an
hour it would get a little darker and deeper each time, but you
should do it by yourself by now.

Well, that is just like any sad dance. You have to give it an inner
significance. Don't just bury a little dead bird in the middle of
the stage.

Cerebralism

Cerebralism is a term describing the dehumanization of art. It refers not only to the use of mental processes, but defines a point of view and an objective. The reaction from the emotional and sentimental morass into which the arts had descended in the late Nineteenth Century swung the first art revolutionaries violently from the previous overindulgence of feeling toward an ordered, calculated unsentimentality. The work of art was dehumanized in so far as it was possible; it was drawn away from biological concepts and found its principles of presentation in the purism of the geometrical and mechanical. Nothing was to be done from the heart; all was from the mind. Although the violence of disgust with the Romantic has expended itself somewhat by now, the conceptions of all the modernists are universally away from personal emotional outpourings, and toward a world which is governed by physical laws — a world especially conscious of the physical properties of space, of volume, of weight, of time, of light.

In the early part of this century the machine served as the symbol of motion without emotion. The Twenties saw the peak of a calculated stylization of the arts which was brought to life through methods influenced by the machine and by science. Each art expressed the new cerebral point of view in a different way, but all embraced it with vigor.

Musicians abandoned the diatonic modes and wrote atonally; that is, each note of the twelve in the octave was independent of any tonality with the other eleven. No three consecutive notes were used which would suggest a tonality. With this twelve tone scale the possibilities of variation in harmony are unlimited, but the unifying base for a composition which had been provided by a consistent key was lost. Schoenberg originated a new constructive device which he called the twelve tone set or row, in which a predetermined relationship between the twelve tones is sustained throughout one piece. Atonal writing has a jagged, biting quality which seems

twelve tone row used by Wallingford Riegger

to be the language needed to express the tensions and sharp colors of this century. Its dissonances have called forth all the epithets available from a startled listening public accustomed to tonic writing. But it should be remembered that dissonance is a comparative term. A chord is pronounced dissonant according to the harmonic context to which the ear of the listener is conditioned. Today's atonality is successfully used to express a mood, even though, at first, the composer's aim was to abandon any emotional flavor. Another feature of contemporary musical composition is the return to a use of counterpoint (now termed "free counterpoint"). Its less complex sound vibrations are not as emotion-arousing as homophonic music.

In architecture the ideal of beauty became a strictly formal, functional one, achieved through geometrical shapes — clean of line and cool of emotion. The Cubist painters, although their broken forms derived from the planalism of the archaic

Three Women — Fernand Leger
Courtesy, Museum of Modern Art, New York
Mrs. Simon Guggenheim Fund

style, were also cerebral. Cubism represented space according to mental conceptions, not by the old optical standards. The non-representational purism of the abstractionist painters like Mondrian is obvious. Jackson Pollock's non-objective canvases are suggestive not of human forms but of the physicist's macrocosm. Even Surrealism, which is thought to be illustrative of subconscious emotion, by the act of consciously using subjective material implies a complete detachment — an objectivity which is clinical. Alexander Calder's mobiles float through space with the poetry of motion, not emotion.

Plays with mechanized action like RUR, The Adding Machine, had a great vogue, and the constructivists were the most looked-to stage designers. In the early years of Russian Bolshevism, when all the traditional habits of life had been overturned, a radically different theatre sprang up. The Meyerhold Theatre, state supported, succeeded in unifying acting and settings and accompanying sounds through a style of Constructivism. The stage (in the round) was set with purely functional platforms and ladders, ramps and scaffoldings, which forced movement in space upon the players. The actors were dehumanized by treating them merely as symbols or mouthpieces for the poet's ideas; the costuming was abstract — sometimes the whole cast was dressed in coveralls. The dryness of this type of performance gave it short life, but its daring created excited interest all over Europe, and led to the so-called skeletal stage designs of today (such as Joe Mielziner's Death of a Salesman set) which gave the audience a sort of X-ray vision.

When Edith Sitwell gave a public reading of her poems, Façade, she devised a way to dehumanize the occasion by remaining invisible, delivering the lines through a megaphone which formed the mouth of a painted clown on the drop curtain. In Notes on My Poetry she unhesitatingly "explains" metaphors, and refers to her word choices as "experiments." This is a

TWA Terminal at Idlewild International Airport
Architects: Eero Saarinen & Associates
Exhibition: Arhitecture and Imagery — Four New Buildings
Feb. 11-April 19, 1959, Museum of Modern Art, New York

far cry from the proverbial Victorian poet who waited, re-
ceptive, for his Muse to beckon. Gertrude Stein converts
words into playthings in the following passage from The First
Reader:

> Halve biscuits and have biscuits. Have to have
> biscuits. Have to halve biscuits. And have to have
> half a biscuit. Just think how to drink lemonade and
> have payed to have a biscuit or to have bread.

Today this taste for Constructivism and abstract design is
still very strong, showing itself everywhere in our commer-
cial products — furniture, wallpaper, fabrics, printing lay-
outs — and even in our human relationships: people, too, are
manipulated like statistics. Sentimentality is out of style.
No young lover would think of kneeling before the lady of his
heart's choice to propose marriage. We "debunk" everything:
tear away the gloss; aim straight at the hard reasonable fact.
The great dramatic moments of modern history are known as
"D Day," "VJ Day." Our greatest political invention is known
only as the "UN." What an unimaginable possibility to think
of the founding fathers referring to the Declaration of Inde-
pendence as the "D. O. I. !"

The coldness of purely surface design and its denial of any
human element represents an escape from the confused e-
motions of modern men, and so we instinctively feel a satisfaction in its purity and clarity. We delight in qualities of
formalism and control. Witness the rediscovery and popularity, during the last forty years, of Bach after a scornful
neglect of his "dry as dust" style during the romantic period.

An excessive dependence on the cerebral to define our aesthetic ideas can lead to sterility and to vacuity. Many critics
have accused the abstractionists of an escapism from life —
an inability to face the puzzling complexities of human problems. Recognizing the aridity and coldness which lie in extreme abstraction, artists of today have modified their use

of the principles of Cerebralism. There is certainly the tendency still to dehumanize, but in the geometric, mechanized pattern there lies much feeling and reference to human emotions — the beginning of a neo-romantic art.

DANCE STUDY IN CEREBRALISM

To build a dance in this vein, the student should devise movement patterns which aim only to create a geometric space design. The cerebral choreographic study avoids all living forms and denies any personal emotions. It debunks sentiment. It depends on a conscious mechanical and abstract manipulation of space and rhythm — on geometrical and mechanical motions. With the painters and sculptors of the constructivist school, space is elevated to a mystical element. So also the cerebral dance study uses space as a medium in which to carve out on mechanical principles a pattern of meticulously accurate movement.

A scheme of movement must be decided upon. The following choreographic ideas can be experimented with, in addition to the obvious one of stylizing the movement of a machine or a mechanized gadget. The dancer can take symbols, levels, geometrical shapes — can enlarge, vary, invert; transpose in bodily movement the shapes of letters, of numbers, of initials, of punctuation marks, or the outline of any inanimate object. Variations can be made on a quality of movement (percussive or staccato); on a direction (diagonals in the parts of the body and the floor pattern); on a tempo of movement (for instance, slow-motion). At the same time it must be remembered that a catalogue is not an art expression. These abstract patterns must develop into a form with a distinguishable and unified structure: a beginning, a middle and an end. They must make a dance.

The body is used with a maximum of depersonalization. (Depersonalization can be augmented by the use of masks or abstract props). The movement is unnatural, without heart or feeling. Everything is line. Of course, the dancer can never express the completely abstract, because the instrument he uses is inescapably human. For instance, a study using the shape of the letters SOS for its form could be a dance which might also suggest fear.

This type is especially adaptable to the humorous, because the anomaly of the human body behaving unhumanly is automatically funny when carried to an extreme. Sybil Shearer's composition, In a Vacuum stirs in the audience pity for the poor unfortunates who must plod through stupid and empty lives, but it is performed with a ludicrous detachment and mechanical indifference.

"Finials" from Allegory — Choreography by Alwin Nikolais
Danced by Murray Louis and Beverly Schmidt
Photograph by David S. Berlin

TANZ UND SPIELSTÜCKE
op. 40

Ernst Toch

Jazz

Jazz is a sort of popular primitivism, illustrating in its sensual moods, tempi and pulses the desire of our sophisticated and complex culture to return to the rhythm and body movements of a less civilized society. It is the folk dance of the Twentieth Century. As with other Twentieth Century phenomena, its rapidity of development and infectious invasion of all parts of the world has been without precedent. The history of jazz covers little more than fifty years, but its influence on the present arts of dance and music is undeniably important.

The original seed of our present pervading form, of course, was imported to America with the primitive culture of the African slaves. Their native music was then adapted to hymns, songs, marches, which the Negroes were exposed to after their transplantation. And so the form has grown, almost completely unintellectualized, through the Spiritual, the Cake Walk, Rag Time, Dixieland, Swing, and now, Rock 'n Roll and Modern or Progressive Jazz. It does not imitate the typical ethnic African, but it retains many of the attributes brought from Africa: jerky, percussive movements and accents. It displays qualities of syncopation which grew out of a disintegrated people: a melancholy and lassitude, resultant of slavery. Its evolution has carried it from song, to dance accompaniment, to Modern Jazz, which is purely a popular concert form, but it remains vital and many-faceted and highly inventive.

Although jazz is by now cosmopolitan and international, and has proved its affinity to the whole modern world by its popularity with all races and cultures, still it is most typically American. It is natural to all Americans, as deeply and subconsciously understood as any other folk dance is understood by the people from whom it grew. It is specifically the expression of present-day urban America. It is an intimate part of our daily life and shows in the urban walk, the posture, the rhythm of speech, the gesture, the costumes, of the city. It belongs to a certain way we have of standing — a slouch, one hip thrown out — of sitting in an informal sprawl, of speaking in slangy abruptness. Jazz is the trade mark of the city.

All kinds of modern artists, especially composers and dancers, have used jazz in their serious work. It has a quality of unpretentious directness which arises from its closeness to people's feelings and instinctive ways of expressing themselves. It certainly bears traces of its African origins, but its distinctive features today show that it has travelled far beyond that ancestry. Polyrhythmic composition is not new; we know it in madrigals and many varieties of primitive music. The special excitement of jazz is produced by clashing two definitely and regularly marked rhythms. Milhaud has said that jazz hit the music world "like a beneficent thunderclap which cleared the art sky." Because in the beginning its devotees were for the most part unschooled in academic music and because its development has been largely through improvisation, its inventions have an honesty of form about them which has provided rich material for the "serious" composer's use.

Writers everywhere are experimenting with the challenging variety of its rhythmic patterns, and embracing to some extent its flavor of nervous, even hysterical high tension. Other musical devices have been adapted with enriching success; devices from "hot" jazz: very elaborate syncopation and percussion (an inheritance from jungle drums) and from "blues": the "wah wah," and "smear," the wail of the lugubrious legato. Some serious writers do more than adapt it; they compose directly in jazz forms: Copland, Bernstein, Gershwin, Gruenberg. In the theatre the jazzy tempo of urban American life

Three Girls on Subway Platform — Etching by Reginald Marsh
Courtesy of Kennedy Galleries, Inc., New York

REGINALD MARSH 1930

Reginald Marsh (F.M)

is the base of such plays as Elmer Rice's <u>Street Scene</u>, <u>Dead End</u> of Sidney Kingsley, Saroyan's <u>The Beautiful People</u>, and certain of the musicals: <u>Guys and Dolls</u>, <u>West Side Story</u>, etc. In the happy marriage of the typically American theme with this typically American music which comprises the Broadway musical, many people see promise of a truly new art form.

Jazz subjects of city life distinguish the work of many American painters. Others, although completely abstract in their manner, plainly echo the syncopated rhythms and violent colors of jazz music.

Literature not only has had its subject matter shaped by the violence, the joylessness of city life, but for certain purposes poets compose directly in a jazz lingo and rhythm. Langston Hughes in a poem called <u>The Cat and the Saxophone</u> (2 A. M.), writes in the syncopated, percussive accents of jazz:

EVERYBODY
Half-pint, —
gin?
No, make it
LOVES MY BABY
corn. You like
liquor,
don't you, honey?
BUT MY BABY
Sure. Kiss me,
DON'T LOVE NOBODY
daddy.
BUT ME.
Say!
EVERYBODY
Yes?
WANTS MY BABY
I'm your
BUT MY BABY

sweetie ain't I?
DON'T WANT NOBODY
Sure.
BUT
Then let's
ME,
do it!
SWEET ME.
Charleston
Mamma!
!

We speak of the "jazz tempo." This suits our American temperament (exciting, given to extremes) and any contemporary urban subject suits this tempo. The modern dancer is always a little jazzy in his typical vigorous and primitive movement, but it is useful for him to analyze characteristics of the popular forms in order to be able to build them into an aesthetic expression.

There are different types of jazz in music and dance, the slow drag: the blues in which the movement is languorous, "cool," "oozy," "snake hips," shuffling feet — a descendant of the melancholy spiritual of the southern Negro; and the "hot" jazz: high-stepping, feverish, hysterical, the Shimmy, the Jitterbug, Bebop, residing in the high tension and hectic scramble of city life. Along with its exaggerated and intoxicated rhythms there is a certain posture and use of the body which is typical of either: a slouched back, negligent throw of the arms, relaxed joints, swinging hips, shrugging shoulders. In its popular form it has an effortless, improvisational quality, and no rigid form. Its extreme physicality brings it close to the modern dance. In contrast to the unearthly aura which the ballet strives for, its movements emanate basically in the pelvic area and often appear sensual and sometimes sexual. Jazz is tense in its driving insistence, and at the same time relaxed in its informality. Jazz musicians, even though they

Visa 1951 — Stuart Davis
Courtesy, Museum of Modern Art.
Gift of Mrs. Gertrud A. Mellon

may play loud and very fast, possess a special relaxed and detached manner quite different from the concentrated attention of the symphony player.

DANCE STUDY IN JAZZ

The jazz dance study should not be a direct imitation of the source forms — not a Harlem scene or a Honky Tonk routine. The style is used to present the flavor of American city life. The jazz posture, typical of the Twentieth Century American, and off-beat movements borrowed from the successive ragtime and jazz popular dances, Bunny Hug, Shimmy, Charleston, Blackbottom, Jitterbug, Rock'n Roll, etc. — should provide the rhythm, the line, and the dynamics to make a dance of city frustrations, tensions, humor, or of a romantic lyric idea suggested by such titles as Gas House Nocturne, Desire Under the El, 10th Avenue Idyll. The problem is to use the jazz dance feeling but to put it into an aesthetic pattern.

Some familiar words, expressions and song titles should stir in the dance student memory of movement which will reflect the style: "moanin' low," "hot diggetty dog," "lonesome blues," "cool cat," "groovey," "The Troubles Ah've Seen." But it should never be forgotten that there must be a form into which the qualities and style can be arranged if the dance is to have choreographic validity.

Strange Hero — Daniel Nagrin   Photograph by Marcus Blechman

III

Blair Fairchild

Mr. Horst Criticizes Dance Studies in JAZZ

I didn't feel the aura of city life.
You need a little more characterization — a gangster's moll or
anything you want to do.

                    The middle part is too long and too
                    slow. You've got to keep that going.

Maybe you'll say, "This is corny." But all jazz is corny.

                    It calls for a repeat.
                    Otherwise we don't
                    know what's going on.

You got there one count too soon.

You can't just be a playful girl, playing and rolling
around on the floor. Jazz is a little sensual.
Throw out your hips!

                    Frankly, you supposedly jazz babies will never get to it.
                    I'm trying to get you to be a little more jazzy - - - - - -

Americana

The study of this style, although not a universal one, is important for dancers to absorb because its qualities are just those which make the modern dance in this country distinguished as the Modern American dance. It expresses the extension, the out-going, expanded movement typical of the American, whether he is dancing or just walking or talking. It was born of our land, our kind of people, and our early history. It is still fresh with the vitality of our formative years and continues everywhere as the conviction of an "American way of life." It arose in rural America, but in some degree resides in all of us.

In this country the first true republic of modern times was established: "the land of the free," "God's country." The huge resources of the land gave every man an opportunity. He was his own boss, dependent on his own initiative; and today he clings unthinkingly to the American ideal of personal liberty.

In the American scene there have been no peasants. The rural folk are independent farmers, ranchers, or rangers. The closed-in, restricted people of Europe came here to expand in the "great open spaces," to respond to the beckoning richness of the land, and push out farther and farther the frontiers. We still feel nostalgia for camping, for the cowboy figure.

The city's children become Camp Fire Girls and Boy Scouts, studying lore of the woods.

The typical American has a lust to move, to go, to look for new frontiers. This is the drive that Martha Graham projected with such vividness in her solo, <u>Frontier</u>. Walt Whitman sings of <u>The Open Road</u>. Emerson writes "Hitch your wagon to a star." We describe the bright young man's prospects with the phrase "he's going places." We are always looking for "more elbow room." Our gaze is focused "way out yonder," or "to hell and gone." Every aspect of our ideal is big; from the unlimited horizon, to the energy of the people (the Paul Bunyan myth). The American type is known to have inclinations toward bragging and boasting; he is given to "tall tales" and "spread eagle speeches."

The "100% American" is direct and homely and proud of his simpleness, his straightforwardness. In revolt against the effete artificiality of Europe, the early settlers worshipped the honest, the open, the plain. We are quick to make friends, loud and informal — "just plain folks," "straight shooters." The "cracker barrel philosophy" of rural America is one of "horse sense," of natural perspicacity without much "book learnin'." It is proud of its "home-spun" language. True to the archetype "Honest Abe," the popular political figure is usually "a man of the people." We even recognize physical attributes typical of the rural American — long-legged girls, rangy men, the slow-moving, speech-drawling, long-striding figure — especially in our Tennessee and Kentucky mountaineers and Western cowboys.

Walt Whitman, overflowing with the energy, the optimism of America, appointed himself the mouthpiece for the philosophy of the New World. His verse form was daringly free in rhythm and rhyme.

John Brown — John Steuart Curry
Courtesy of The Metropolitan Museum of Art, New York
Arthur H. Hearn Fund, 1950

Those of the open atmosphere, coarse, sunlit,
    fresh, nutritious,
Those that go their own gait erect, stepping with freedom
    and command — leading, not following,
Those with never-quell'd audacity — those with sweet
    and lusty flesh, clear of taint,
Those that look carelessly in the faces of Presidents
    and Governors, as to say, "Who are you?"
Those of earth-born passion, simple, never constrain'd,
    never obedient,
Those of inland America.

                (from The Prairie-Grass Dividing)

Until recently, suspicious of our own taste, we insisted upon looking to Europe for "culture." Walt Whitman was probably the first to stir America to the realization of her own indigenous beauty and spirit. The Regional Painters — Curry, Benton and Wood — and the novelist, Sinclair Lewis, emphasized a new ideal of subject matter. Now artists in every field have ceased to consider study in Europe a necessity. Frank Lloyd Wright, with the smell of the Wisconsin farm land (where he worked as a boy) in his nostrils, wanted his buildings "...to come out of the ground into the light — the ground itself held always as a component part of the building itself." His designs were shaped by the Western plains and the political climate of the democracy to which he belonged.

The expansive, free approach which an American takes for granted, is striking to the European. A critic for the newspaper Candido of Milan in reporting on the American paintings at the Biennale in Venice, 1956, spoke of "enormously extended and strangely lit perspectives," and added "American artists still struggle with the immediacy and the power which beats on their door. This is why even the abstract and semi-abstract artists seem to us more convincing." No

Frontier — Martha Graham   Photograph by Barbara Morgan

lengthy explanation of this style is necessary for the American reader. It is drawn upon constantly by American dancers of every category. Typical are Graham's <u>Frontier</u> with its Louis Horst score, and <u>Appalachian Spring</u>, DeMille's <u>Rodeo</u> and dances from <u>Oklahoma!</u>, Eugene Loring's <u>Billy the Kid</u>, and Balanchine's <u>Western Symphony</u>.

DANCE STUDY IN AMERICANA

The dance exercise in this mood is one of big, free and extended movement. The design should reach into surrounding wide open spaces that are clearly implied by the expanding gestures. Every gesture is direct, honest and without adornment. It is swinging and out-going — a wide stance in the legs and an open carriage of the chest.

Dance ideas should grow out of images suggested in the preceding discussion. Sometimes the sentimentality which is heavy in folk songs or popular songs like "The Trail of the Lonesome Pine," or "They Buried Her in the Old Prairie," "Sunbonnet Sue," etc., can create the style if handled with good taste and a sense of form. The friendly gaiety and informal simplicity of the square dance is one strong source of choreographic material which will elaborate this theme.

The expansive movement that can fill and reach beyond a stage is natural to the American dancer's body. It is in every American's blood. It is our signature. With it a great many contemporary ideas, not necessarily on national themes, can be put into concert dance form.

Square Dances — Doris Humphrey and Charles Weidman
Photograph by Barbara Morgan

Sheep and Goat
"Walkin' to the Pasture"

David W. Guion

Gaily, with marked swing and rhythm, though not too fast

Piano

Mr. Horst Criticizes Dance Studies in AMERICANA

You get too movey, too leggy. It's overdoing it a little, especially for the sentimental aspect of rural America. There should have been moments of quiet, and not too much pyrotechnics going on all the time.

It isn't enough just to stretch out the arms. You have to give that little extra thing — that way-out-yonder flavor, so that we feel we forget that wall there. It's tension rather than spread.

Move with audacity into space.

It's not quite free wheeling enough. You had a lot of good movements, but it gets to be a little too much. You don't have to keep jumping around all the time.

We always want breadth. This comes out better if you're facing us.

We in America have a wider step. When I was in Paris there was a parade of the Allied troops, American marches are always played slower than French marches because the French take shorter steps. American soldiers come striding along.

Impressionism

Impressionism is not strictly an immediacy of modern life. It preceded in time the deep change brought with Freudian psychology, and the full force of the cerebralism of a mechanical age. However, its style and ideals are still factors in the contemporary creative arts. They are of especial significance to the dancer if he wishes to express lyric and poetic themes without forsaking the desire to avoid sentimentality. This article on Impressionism has only been placed after the pupil has grappled with the problems of the other "Immediacies" because of the extreme difficulty in applying its special characteristics to composition in movement.

Impressionism fell heir to its name in 1867 through a derogatory comment made by an art critic when writing of Claude Monet's then shocking painting entitled "Impression: Rising Sun." By the 70's the ideals and philosophy of the movement were spreading out from the little group of painters in Paris who first championed them, and were starting to displace moribund romantic forms in all the arts.

Growing trust in science to solve all man's problems influenced the painters to take a scientific attitude toward painting. What was a visual image? What did light have to do with it? How could paint give the effect of light as vibration? In other arts, too, the emphasis shifted onto the material approach: how to use the paint, how to combine the musical notes, what effects could be gotten from words as sounds, apart from their meaning? Dramatic subject matter was less important to what was declared to be "the new realism" than surface effectiveness. The elements of form (structure, organization) were subordinated to the immediate, sensory communication.

Houses of Parliament, Westminster — Claude Monet
Courtesy of The Art Institute of Chicago, Mr. and Mrs. Martin A. Ryerson Collection

The intention of the Impressionists, liberated in every field of art from the slavery to academic rote, was to depict a fleeting, momentary aspect of material nature. There were no great heights and depths, no great suffering or distress. Their aims demonstrated an externalization which followed materialistic modes of thought. The intentions were realized by creating effects which, although brought about with different devices, were quite similar in painting, music, sculpture, poetry.

Even though the impressionist style represented an impassioned reaction to the stilted forms of romanticism, still it carried over some of the romantic attitude to its novel techniques. The feeling is elusive, blurred, tenuous, hazy, like out-of-focus photography. It radiates a sort of vibrancy and luminosity. Because depth and organization were neglected and the presentation of the material fragmented, there is a characteristic lack of form. This weakness caused Cezanne to leave the Impressionists in impatience and work out his own great rules of structure — the intermediate step to Cubism.

The impressionistic view of art, although it was accepted throughout the world and had its effect in all directions, was nurtured and flourished especially in France. The painters attained the vibrating, shimmering effect by the now very familiar technique of breaking colors into their primary elements. The paints were applied in juxtaposition on the canvas so that they were mixed in the eye of the viewer instead of on the palette. The interest was principally in light and its effect on real objects. Monet was perhaps the purest Impressionist in his consistently broken color and his way of ignoring form. Seurat's distinctly placed figures are monumental in spite of the pointillist technique of applying paint, but always cool and removed in their comment. The immediately endearing world of Renoir's painting is typical of the poetic radiance of the whole impressionist school.

The Symboliste poets, Rimbaud, Mallarmé, Verlaine, Valéry and others, wrote mood-evoking, diffuse, cryptic, impersonal poetry in the last quarter of the Nineteenth Century in Paris. Their subjects were of nature rather than of man, the surface of things rather than inner qualities. They sought words which of themselves would convey emotional, nonintellectual impressions like the broken-up colors of the Impressionist painters and the shimmering note combinations of the musicians; words which lost any definite meaning and dissolved into symbols. The mellifluous sound of the French language lends itself to the intention of the Symboliste poetry, but by its very nature that poetry is almost untranslatable. Brian Hill does succeed in reproducing the mood of Verlaine's descriptive poem by transposing alliterations and nostalgic non-definite connotations from French into English:

> Setting Suns
> A faint dawn slowly
> Spills on the dunes
> The melancholy
> Of setting suns;
> And melancholy
> Lulls with sweet tunes
> My heart lost wholly
> In setting suns.
> Strange fancies lure,
> Like suns that slide
> To the ocean's shore.
> Wraiths rosy-dyed
> Gliding evermore;
> Like suns they glide
> Great suns that slide
> To the ocean's shore.

Because of its limited scope the Symboliste movement led to a dead end, but its many discoveries are used by all writers today. The Imagists, too, a group of poets in England and

America, who held the floor in the 1920's, seem now to be "dated." They wrote poetry of the physical senses rather than the soul, selecting each word with scientific exactitude for its visual and auditory effect. Like the Impressionists, the only structure was a relation between images.

<u>Oread</u>
Whirl up, sea —
whirl your pointed pines,
splash your great pines
on our rocks,
hurl your green over us,
cover us with your pools of fir.
                    H.D. (Hilda Doolittle)

In music Debussy achieved a new kind of vibrant, liquid texture by some fairly simple harmonic devices, which have been an important influence on subsequent composers. He created a haunting effect by adding a major second (what came to be known as Debussy's vibrant second) above the tonic of the major triad. And a still more liquid effect was achieved by also adding a major second above the dominant.

major triad   second above   plus second above
                     the tonic   the dominant

Typical of Debussy's writing is his adaptation of the whole tone, pentatonic and other modal scales to supplement the diatonic which had been the basis of composition since the Renaissance.

GOD SAVE THE KING played in different modes

Characteristically, he would move his voices in parallel motion instead of opposition, thus leaving chords suspended, that is, active tones unresolved. The shimmer we associate with his music was created by overtones as he moved from key to key without modulation. Such harmonic innovations, which sound soft and nostalgic to our ears, were considered shocking and unpleasantly discordant in Debussy's time. The titles of his compositions — Clouds, Reflections in the Water, Footsteps in the Snow, Garden in the Rain, suggest immediately the mood-making, liquid quality of the music.

In the field of sculpture the Impressionists were concerned with the sensual play of light on their figures. Rodin's stippled or broken surfaces were used to obtain a "brilliant luminosity" on the exterior of his sculpture.

In the theatre the urge toward fragmentation manifested itself in plays with a frequently changing locale of action. Maeterlinck's Pelléas and Melisande, written in 1892, has five acts and within them are included twenty scenes. This

constantly shifting focus for the action is typically impressionistic, and made the play an ideal libretto for Debussy's
opera.

The impetus which resulted from discoveries of the Impressionists is still an important force, but the form itself was
too fragmentary and too lacking in virility to lead into further
developments. In its pure form it is now looked upon as a
document recording the scientific, empirical world of that
time. Impressionism's intrinsically narrow view became
mannered and specialized after a time and finally faded into
a state of anemia. But the original contribution that it made
was enormous, and the techniques it invented to arrive at
certain effects are of constant service to the dancer. Impressionism proceeded to Post-Impressionism, a style which
led into Twentieth Century art.

DANCE STUDY IN IMPRESSIONISM

Because the Impressionist manner is a formless one, the
style is the most difficult of all for the dancer to work in and
to adapt effectively. Only the fairly experienced choreographer should attempt its subtle delicacies of suggestion.
He will have to sacrifice definiteness of structure, but at the
same time must compose as strictly as always (the form is
not improvisational) with the most tenuous of foundations
upon which to build.

In order to compose with movement and a pattern which will
evoke the impressionist mood, the dancer must think mainly
of fragmentation. One movement is interrupted by another
(even a change while the body is in the air). One gesture is
broken into by another, or perhaps left unfinished. Direction
is constantly being varied like Debussy's changing tonalities;
the focus turns this way and that way — even to a shifting eye.

Lilac Garden — Choreography by Antony Tudor
Danced by — Hugh Laing, Tanaquil LeClerq, Brooks Jackson and Nora Kaye
Courtesy, New York Public Library   Photograph by George Platt Lynes

Frequently altered tempo, abrupt changes in dynamics (from a tense to a relaxed movement, from a slow to a fast or a change in space and pace) contribute to the shimmering, fragmented quality which gives the style its flavor. Although it is impossible for the human body actually to fragment itself, by these devices of interrupted line, texture, and rhythm an effect can be achieved which is similar to the one the painters attained with their broken colors.

One wouldn't do a war dance in the impressionist mood. The style is suitable to lyric subjects which demand poetic atmosphere rather than dramatic situations or actions, to themes of nature: the night, the forest, moving water, etc. Contemporary ideas which are drawn from fantasy, dreams, or unstable, shifting emotions can be made vivid with this mode of movement. The impressionist dance has a romantic tone but still achieves the dissonance that belongs to our time. It arouses an intensity of attention by its very failure to complete, which is hauntingly affecting. The style has been used by contemporary choreographers to create a poetic mood with a modern texture, removed from any specific development of plot such as, Antony Tudor's Lilac Garden, Sybil Shearer's In The Cool of the Garden.

VALSES NOBLES ET SENTIMENTALES
No. 5

Presque lent—dans un sentiment intime ♩ = 96

Maurice Ravel

Conclusion

These principal styles of modern dance expression, as they have been set forth in broad terms, can, at best, be only arrows which may direct the choreographer to appropriate forms in which to couch his ideas. It must be stressed that it has been for the purpose of bringing clear understanding both intellectually and physically that the characteristics of these eight sources of expression have been discussed in so segmented a fashion. Actually they are not eternal and certainly they are not exclusive, nor are they independent.

As foundation for these styles there must be a structure, a framework - not necessarily obvious to the audience, but definite to the composer. It is usually a relative of the basic ABA form. For mature and complex dance works this three part form expands into a freer version, just as it does in symphonic musical writing where it may become A A B B etc. - followed by a C with transitional sections. Flexibility in the very strict form adhered to in the brief and simple studies which the dancer has practiced during his apprenticeship can now be allowed. But always the same eye for compactness and precision must guide the choreographer when making a more pretentious work, in spite of whatever aesthetic license with the strict form he may indulge in. Also, if the composition is a narrative, some of the laws of form can be sacrificed to the specific need of the content — an "irregular form" will serve.

In order to create works of any significance, the choreographer must have, in addition to a thorough working knowledge of form and style, his own background of knowledge and opinion. He must be forever a student and an observer. He should give sharp attention, as the actor does, to the movements and the rhythms of men and women at work and at play, in love, in anger, in fear, in doubt, in stupidity. He should try to understand how and why the behavior of his contemporaries differs from human behavior of other times.

But also he must feed his observations with the culture that is his own inheritance. He must study the records of history, of philosophy, of all the ages behind him. He must particularly continue to investigate for himself the periods that are the special sources for all the modern arts: the primitive, the archaic, the medieval. He will want to be acquainted with the output of painters, musicians, writers of today, through whom he can benefit by a shortcut to understanding the contemporary definition of beauty and scope of subject matter.

All this research and recording in his memory will be resource for the choreographer's work as an artist, as an interpreter and expositor. But he can only learn how to transpose the communications he has to make into bodily movement through devoted practice and experimentation. The dancer can no more discover how to externalize his idea through merely reading a book about it, than a man with a paint box can expect to create a work of art like Cezanne after reading the most explicit and elaborate Skira publication on that master. He himself must do and do and do, until he discovers and nurtures his own sources and terms of expression. Only practice with an intense purpose and self-scrutiny can show him paths to maturity.

The dancer will first have some motivation to compose. His theme will suggest to him a tempo, a rhythm, a structure of presentation. He will analyze the aesthetic elements inherent in his theme. Then his experience from practice in the various styles described, will suggest to him the type of movement which will be the language in which to present that theme.

When he begins to move, his own emotions, quickly responsive to a sensitive physical instrument, will guide him in the construction of his dance. These emotions must be transposed into a form, a significance, which will deliver back to an audience the motivating idea which was their inspiration. Whether the composition be for one figure or for a group of dancers, Goetschius's rules of good composition (page 26), the laws of aesthetic construction, and contemporary modes of expression remain the guides by which the choreographer finds his way.

Four Don'ts in composing dance should haunt every effort the choreographer makes:

Don't rely for effect on technical virtuosity. Virtuosity may be dazzling, and even necessary at times as descriptive material, but it doesn't pass with the critical observer for choreography. The audience should take a high degree of skill in the dancer's body for granted. Technique is always a means, not an end. It is a natural prerequisite to any dancer's composing, because he simply cannot realize his ideas without it. It is his vocabulary.

Don't lean on a dramatic idea. The dance will become a pantomime and the dancer merely a deaf and dumb actor. The material of a narrative must be sublimated and abstracted through allegory or symbolism, withdrawn from the natural.

Don't make the dance too long. No composition should be
longer than it must be of necessity. By choosing music
which is not too long the temptation to pad out the dance
can better be avoided. Virginia Woolf has said, "Pro-
fusion connotes confusion, and confesses to a structural
weakness." Clarity and brevity are jewels.

Don't be unfaithful to your idea in order to make it palatable
to an inexperienced audience. Clarity is always the
aim, but this is brought about by movement which is
essential to the idea, not by compromising to please.

The dancer's world is one of hard work and intensity. It demands sacrifices at every level of achievement. It is also
one which offers the special satisfaction that arises when
concerted forces of the body and the mind and the intuition
are all directed to one act.

LOUIS HORST — A Brief Biography

An epitaph for Louis Horst (1884–1964) might read "music director, composer, and first teacher of formal composition for dancers." He has been labelled "critic and general force for process" (Capezio Award, 1955) as well as mentor, strict disciplinarian, bundle of contradictions, and opinionated ogre by those who knew him best.

A musician, Louis Horst found himself in a dancer's world by chance. An accomplished pianist, at ease in San Francisco's concert and music halls, Horst accepted a temporary assignment as musical director for the Denishawn Dance Company in 1915. At 31, Horst began a lifelong association with America's leading dancers.

After ten years of arduous touring with Denishawn, Horst accompanied Martha Graham's first historic concert in 1926, and continued to compose, accompany, and conduct for her choreographic work until 1948. During this period, Horst established a precedent of composing specifically for dance, producing outstanding scores for Graham's dances *Primitive Mysteries* (1931), *Celebration* (1934), *Frontier* (1935), and *El Penitente* (1940). They performed at the opening of Radio City Music Hall in 1932, the White House in 1936, and the World's Fair in 1937 in the midst of stellar New York seasons, teaching, and college touring. Known as the "pianist saint of the modern dance," Horst worked with virtually every modern dancer on the New York concert scene during this period, accompanying Doris Humphrey, Harald Kruetzberg, Helen Tamiris, and Charles Weidman, as well as Aldolf Bolm, Agnes de Mille, Ruth Page, and many others.

Horst began to teach music in relation to dance at the Neighborhood Playhouse in 1928. In 1934, he became the founding editor of *Dance Observer,* a periodical devoted to modern dance. By 1935, Horst had evolved two courses, *Pre-Classic Dance Forms* and *Modern Dance Forms,* designed for dancers and actors. Introduced in their entirety at the Bennington School of Dance, these studies were soon complimented by *Group Forms* and *Music for the Dance.* Horst wrote nearly 100 scores for dance in his lifetime.

As an influential leader in the modern dance "establishment," Horst continued to insist on solid principles of form and intentional handling of content in his teaching at major institutions such as the American Dance Festival at Connecticut College and the Juilliard School until his death in 1964.

After a half century of work with dancers, Horst said; "The greatest reward was that in all those years I was doing just what I wanted to do, and realizing it all the time — not merely in retrospect. . . . My enthusiasm for the work has been endless — the young all need guidance — especially the talented ones. They do it themselves, really, but they need a tail to their kite."[1]

At the end of his long career, Horst reflected, "I do not prophesy where the dance is going next or who the new great dancer will be. The important thing is, it is going!"[2] He observed, "Modern dance now has a past it can examine. It can have a future."[3]

This classic test, *Modern Dance Forms* places dance as an independent art in relation to the others, by instilling a sense of history, and the possibility for a rich future. Louis Horst's contribution to the field of modern choreography remains unrivaled.

Janet Soares

[1]Pease, Esther, "Epilogue: A Conversation with Louis Horst." *Impulse 1965*, pp. 4–5.
[2]Mansfield, Marjory, "Whither The Modern Dance?" *The Pine Bark*, December 1962, 1.
[3]Pease, *Op. Cit., p. 7.*

Louis Horst explaining a new subject to a class at The Juilliard School, 1961. Photograph by Radford Bascome

SUGGESTED MUSICAL ACCOMPANIMENTS

UNDERSTANDING BY CONTRAST

Strange Space Design (Pentatonic Scale)

Windsperger, Lothar. Kleine Klavierstücke. Op. 37, Vol. 1,
No. 1. "Nordisches Lied." Mainz: Schott's Soehne.

Planal Space Design (Whole Tone Scale)

Windsperger, Lothar. Kleine Klavierstücke. Op. 37, Vol. 1,
No. 20. "Ganztonleiter-Melodie." Mainz: Schott's Soehne.

Dissonance

Windsperger, Lothar. Kleine Klavierstücke. Op. 37, Vol. 1,
No. 4. "Dissonanzen." Mainz: Schott's Soehne.

Asymmetrical Rhythm (5/4 Study)

Satie, Erik "Danse de la Brouette," from Relâche. Paris: Rouart, Lerolle.

THE BACKGROUNDS OF MODERN ART

Earth Primitive

Bartók, Béla. Fourteen Bagatelles. Op. 6, Nos. 1,2,3,5,6. New York:
Boosey and Hawkes.

Kodaly, Zoltan. 9 Klavierstücke. Op. 3, Nos. 1,5. Budapest: Rozsavolgyi.

7 Pièces pour le Piano. Nos. 1,3. New York: Universal Edition.

Air Primitive

Mompou y Dencausse, Federico. Cants Mágics. (Suite) Nos. 1,2,3,4,5.
Madrid: Unión Músical Española.

Charmes. (forms of primitive incantation)
Nos. 1,2,4. Paris: M. Eschig.

Archaic

Satie, Erik. <u>Gymnopédies</u>. Paris: Rouart, Lerolle.

     <u>Trois Gnossiennes</u>. Paris: Rouart, Lerolle.

Religious Medieval

Maleingreau, Paul de.   <u>Préludes à L'Introït</u> (pour orgue sans pédale).
                Paris: Éditions Maurice Senart.
                Suite 1. Le Temps de la Noël
                   No. 6. St. Thomas Martyr.
                Suite 2. Le Temps de Pâques
                   No. 5. Le Jeudi Saint.
                Suite 5. Fêtes de la Vièrge
                   No. 1. Salve Sancta Parens.
                Suite 6. Propre des Saints
                   No. 7. St. Justin Martyr.
                   No. 14. St. Boniface évêque.
                   No. 34. Les Stigmates de St. François.
                Suite 7. Supplement pour Divers Lieux
                   No. 3. S. Benoit-Joseph Labre
                   No. 7. St. Irénée
                   No. 9. S. Stanislas Kostka

Secular Medieval

Anonymous.   <u>Troubadour Song</u>, arranged by Carlos Salzedo.

Koechlin, Charles.   "Chanson du Pêcheur," from <u>Douze Petite Pièces</u>. (Suite)
                Paris: Éditions Maurice Senart.

IMMEDIACIES OF MODERN LIFE

Introspection

Scriabin, Alexander.   <u>Étude</u>. Op. 49, No. 1.
                <u>Prélude</u>. Op. 49, No. 2.
                <u>Danse Languide</u>. Op. 51, No. 4.
                <u>Désir</u>. Op. 57, No. 1.
                <u>Caresse Dansée</u>. Op. 57, No. 2.
                <u>Prélude</u>. Op. 67, No. 1.
                <u>Prélude</u>. Op. 74, Nos. 2, 3, 4. Leipzig: M. P. Belaieff.

Cerebral

Toch, Ernst.   Tanz und Spielstücke. Op. 40, Nos. 2,3,4,5. Mainz: Schott's Soehne.

Schoenberg, Arnold.   Six Little Pieces. Op. 19, No. 2. Vienna: Universal Edition.

Jazz

Copland, Aaron.   Sentimental Melody. (Slow Dance) London: Schott & Co., Ltd.

Fairchild, Blair.   Cinq Chants Nègres. No. 3. Paris: A. Durand.

Gershwin, George.   Three Preludes. New York: Harms.

Gruenberg, Louis.   Six Jazz Epigrams. Op. 30. Vienna: Universal Edition.

Harsanyi, Tibor.   Rythmes. No. 2. Paris: R. Deiss.

Lloyd, Norman.   Blues. New York: Orchesis Publications.

Milhaud, Darius.   Three Rag-Caprices. No. 2. Vienna: Universal Edition.

Americana

Guion, David W.   Sheep and Goat "Walkin' to the Pasture." New York: Schirmer.

Horst, Louis.   Coming 'Round the Mountain, Boys. (Theme and Variation) New York: Orchesis Publications.

Keeney, Wendell.   Mountain Tune. New York: Schirmer.

Niemann, Walter.   The Mississippi Steam-boat's in Sight. Op. 97, No. 1. Munich: Atlantis-Musikverlag.

Nordoff, Paul.   Katie Bell. (Based on the Stephen Foster Song) New York: Associated Music Publishers, Inc.
The Camptown Races. (Based on the Stephen Foster Song) New York: Associated Music Publishers, Inc.

Impressionism

Ravel, Maurice.   Valses Nobles et Sentimentales. Nos. 2,4,5. Paris: A. Durand.

Index

A

Abstractionist, 104
Air Primitive, 60, 63, 65
Allemande, 24
Appalachian Spring, 19, 126
Après-Midi d'un Faune, L', 74
Archaism, 52, 56, 69, 70
Archipenko, Alexander, 33
Asymmetrical Rhythm, 41–42, 44, 86
asymmetry, 32, 33, 34
Auden, W.H., 56

B

Bach, Johann Sebastian, 106
Balanchine, George, 20, 126
ballet, 16
Bartók, Belá, 33, 64
Bauer, Marion, 42 48
Beckett, Samuel, 56, 94
Bell, Clive, 57
Berg, Alban, 43
Bergson, Henri, 14
Billy the Kid, 126

C

Calder, Alexander, 104
Casella, Alfredo, 48
Cezanne, Paul, 26, 70, 132, 141
Chaucer, Geoffrey, 84
Cheney, Sheldon, 52, 89, 90, 98
Composition, rules of, 23, 26
Constructivism, 104, 106, 107
counterpoint, 33, 46, 102
Courante, 24
Cowell, Henry, 41, 43
cubism, 102, 104, 132
Cunningham, Merce, 72

D

Dance, modern American, 121
definition of, 16–22

Dance study, religious medieval, 81
secular medieval, 83–5
Debussy, Claude, 33, 46, 134, 135, 136
changing tonalities, 136
harmonic devices, 134
opera, 136
Deep Song, 65
de Maleingreau, Paul, 81
De Mille, Agnes, 20
Denishawn, 144
design, two-dimensional, 74
Die Minnesanger, 82
Dissonance, 29, 33, 46, 47, 50
dissonant, 33, 50
distortion, rhythmic, 42, 74
Doolittle, Hilda (H.D.), 134
Dostoievsky, Fydor, 91
Duncan, Isadora, 16

E

Earth Primitive, 60, 61, 65
Egyptian art, 74
Emerson, Ralph Waldo, 122
Emperor Jones, 65
expressionist theatre, 92, 98

F

Facade, 104
Faulkner, William, 26
Fokine, Michel, 20
form, elements of, 130
three-part, 24
four-part, 25
structure, 130
organization, 73, 130
fragmentation, 136
"free counterpoint," 102
Freud, Sigmund, 89, 91
influence, 96
psychology, 130
Frontier, 26, 122, 126

SPECIAL OFFER

MUSIC FOR MODERN DANCE FORMS
A Cassette

Narrated, directed, and produced by Janet Mansfield Soares
Elisenda Fabrégas, Pianist

These 32 short piano pieces were selected by Louis Horst, Musical
Director for the Martha Graham Dance Company, to accompany the
introductory choreographic exercises in his book *Modern Dance
Forms*. Included on the 62-minute cassette are compositions by Satie,
Bartok, Ravel, Mompou, Scriabin, Schoenberg, Gershwin, as well as
several by Horst himself.

Contents: Windsperger: *Planal, Bitonal, Pentatonic, Dissonant*; Satie:
Danse de la Brouette, Gnossienne No. 2, Gymnopedies No. 1; Bartok:
Fourteen Bagatelles: Op. 6 No. 1 and No. 5; Mompou: *Cants Magics No.
2 and Charmes No. 1*; Maleingreau: *Stigmatas of St. Francis*; Koechlin:
Song of a Fisherman; Scriabin: *Prelude, Op. 74, No. 2, Danse Languide Op.
51, No. 4, Desir, Op. 57, No. 1*; Toch: *Op. 40, No. 2*; Fairchild: *Jazz Study
No. 3*; Guion: *Sheep and Goat, Walkin' to Pasture*; Ravel: *Waltz No. 5*;
Lazarus: *Gymnopedie*; Hellebrandt: *Troubadour Song*; de la Halle: *Robin
Loves Me*; Schoenberg: *Op. 19, No. 2*; Gershwin: *Prelude No. 2*; Lloyd:
Blues; Horst: Music for a dissonance study, *Hot Sunday, Comin' Round
the Mountain, Boys*; Niemann: *Op. 97, No. 1: The Mississippi Steamboat's
in Sight*; Paumann: *Religious Medieval*.

You may charge your order with Visa, MasterCard or
American Express from 8:30-4:30 EST at our toll-free number
1-800-220-7149

Or, you can mail in a check or money order for $15.00 to:

Princeton Book Company, Publishers
PO Box 57, Pennington, NJ 08534
(Please make clear that you are ordering the *Music for Modern Dance Forms*
cassette, and include the address to which you want it shipped.)